Great Smoky MOUNTAINS

Wonder and Light

Photography by

Bill Lea, Jerry Greer and Nye Simmons

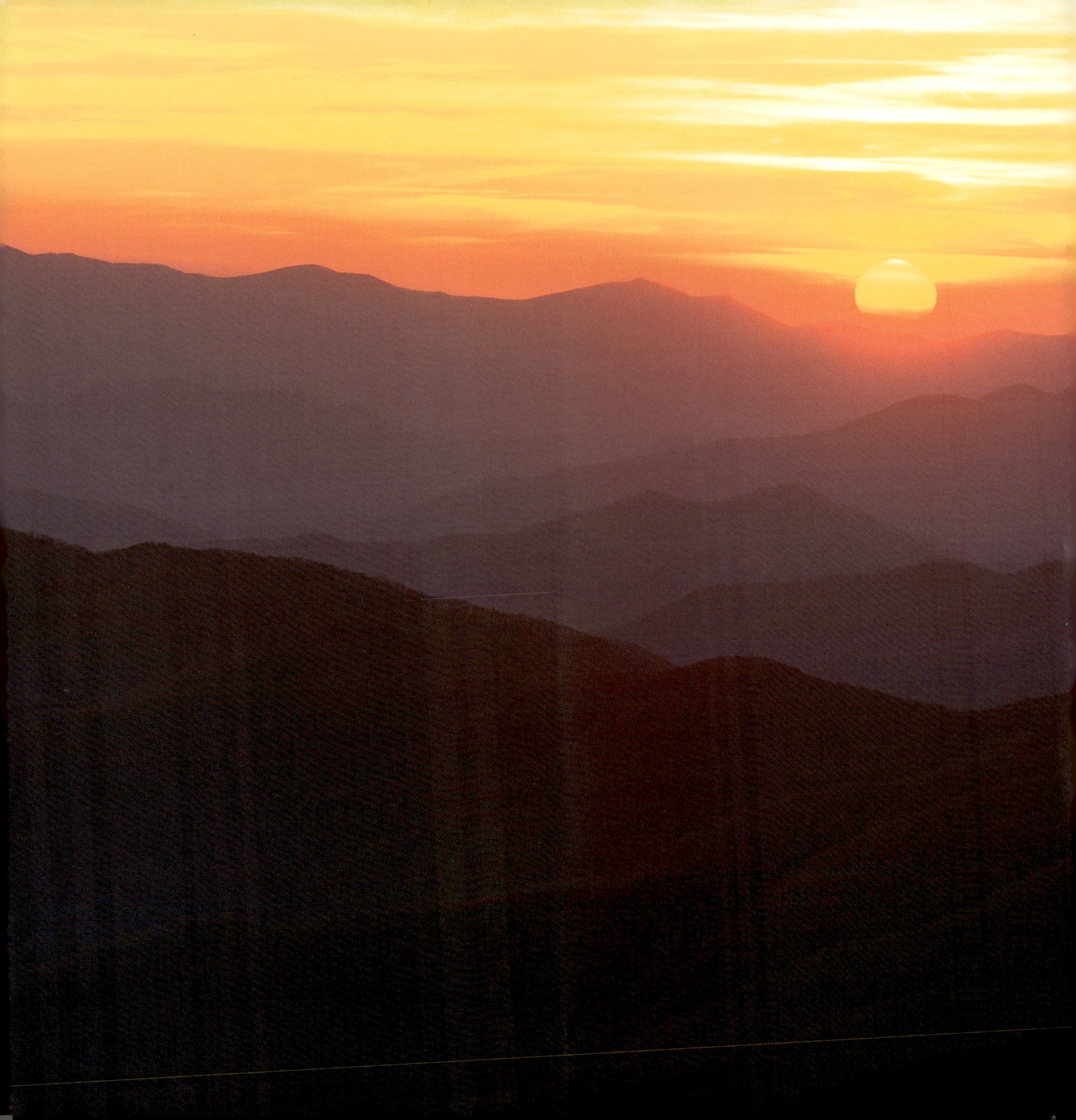

Great Smoky MOUNTAINS

Wonder and Light

Photography by

Bill Lea

Jerry D. Greer

Nye Simmons

Mountain Trail Press

1818 Presswood Road • Johnson City, Tennessee 37604

www.mountaintrailpress.com

Celebrating America's Most Scenic Places

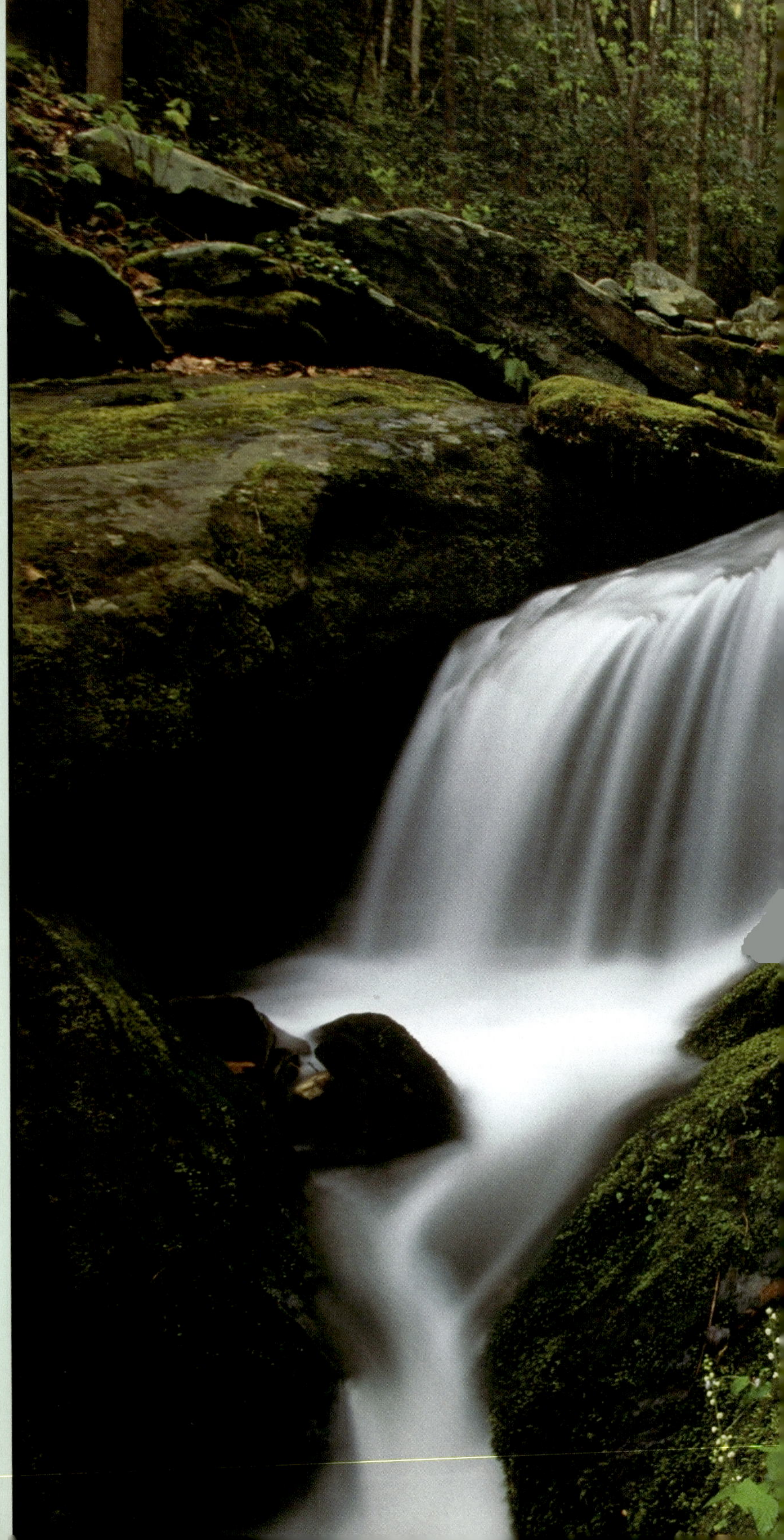

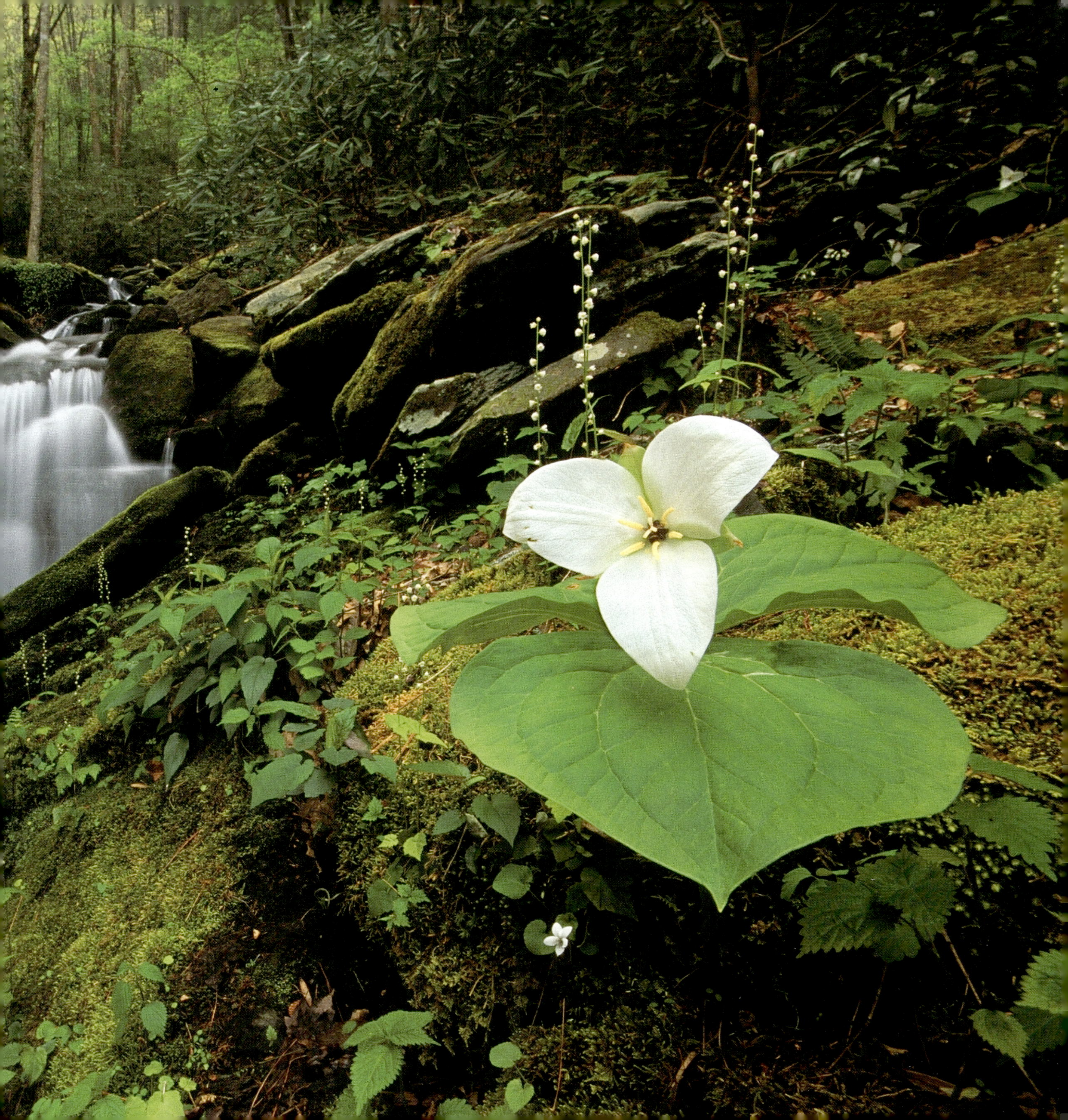

Great Smoky MOUNTAINS

Wonder and Light

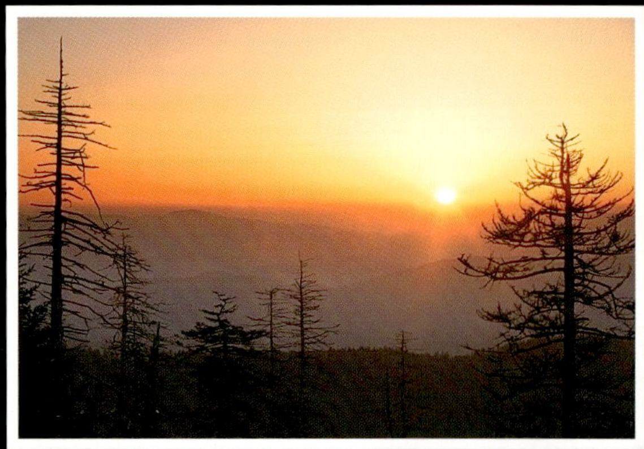

Bill Lea, Jerry Greer and Nye Simmons

Book design: Ian J. Plant
Editor: Jerry D. Greer

Published by Mountain Trail Press LLC
1818 Presswood Road
Johnson City, TN 37604

ISBN: 0-9770808-9-7
Printed in Korea
First Printing, Fall 2006

Front cover: Sunrise from Mount Le Conte (Jerry Greer).

First frontispiece: Crepuscular rays over the Great Smoky Mountains at sunset create a dramatic light show (Bill Lea).

Full page spread: The soft tones of dusk settle over the Great Smoky Mountains, as viewed from Clingmans Dome (Nye Simmons).

Preceding page: Trillium blooms along the many streams of the Smokies in spring (Bill Lea).

Right: A black bear pauses to survey its surroundings (Bill Lea).

Above: Sunrise as seen from Clingmans Dome (Jerry Greer).

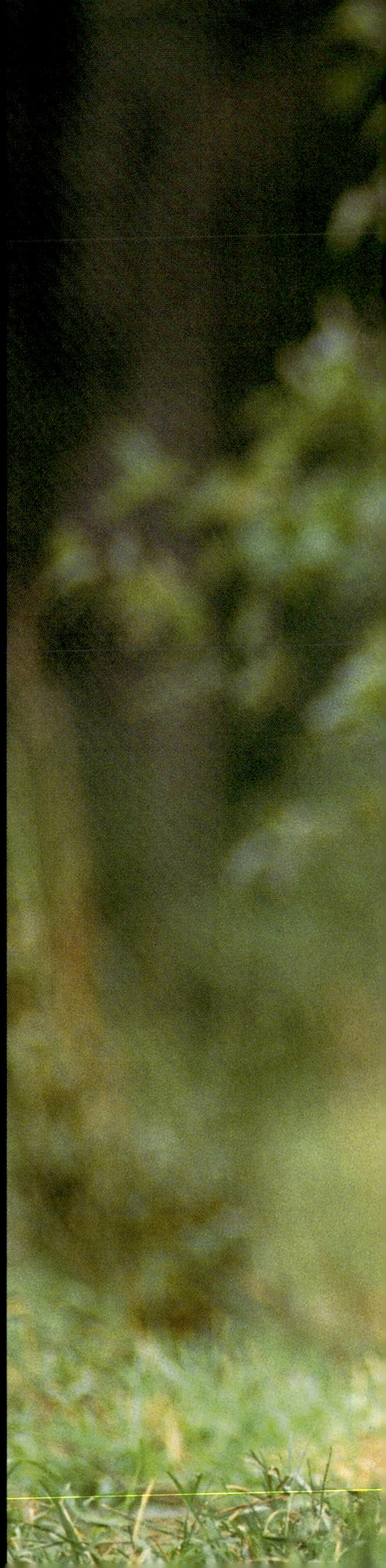

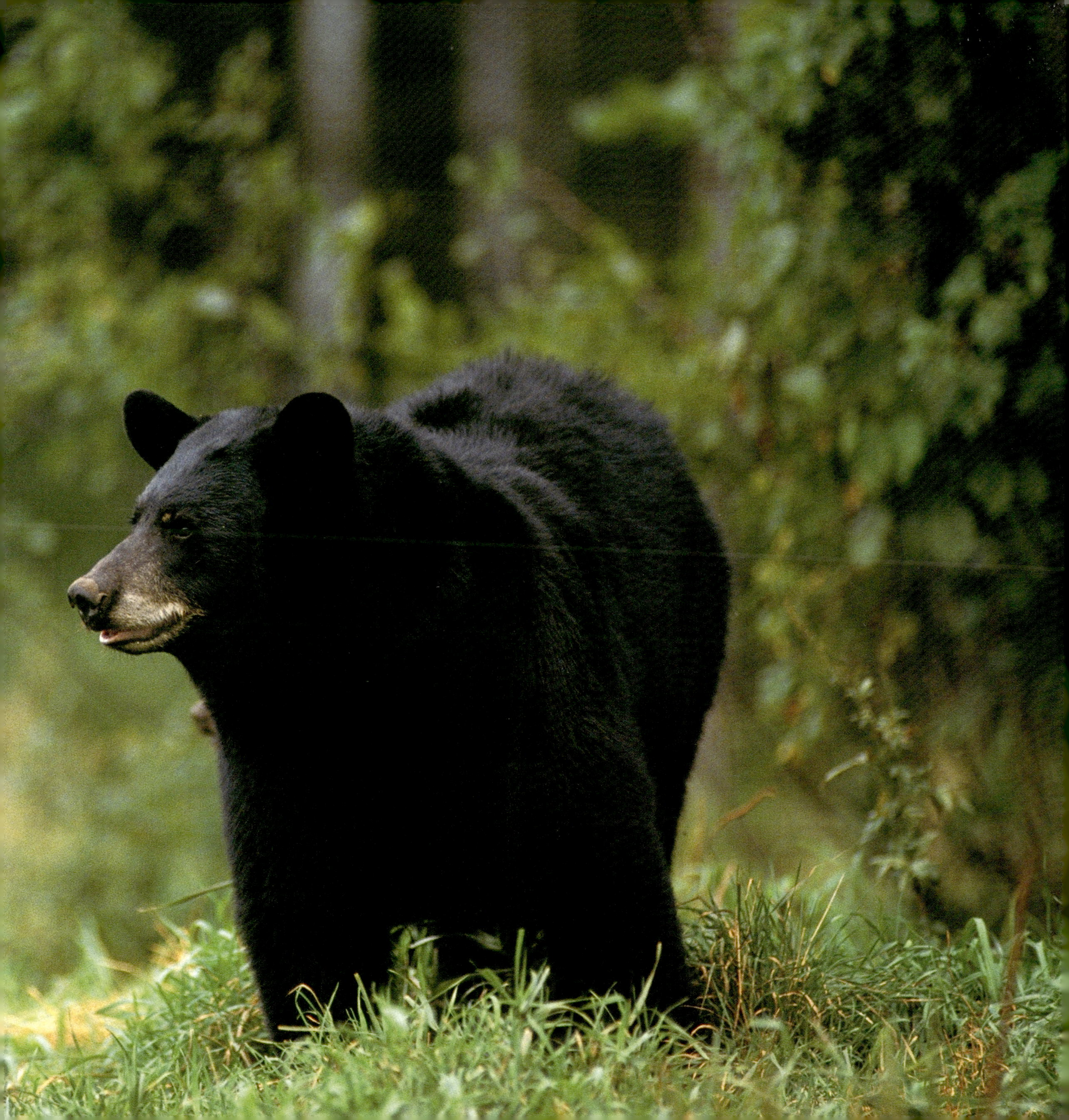

WHAT IMAGES come to mind when you think of the Great Smoky Mountains? Mountains as far as the eye can see? A stream or waterfall? A carpet of wildflowers? A pioneer cabin? Or maybe a black bear? For many of us, the answer is probably "yes" to all of these things and much more!

When I think of the Smokies the word "ancient" comes to mind. Unlike the sharp peaks of the much younger Colorado Rockies or Denali in Alaska, time and weather have softened and rounded the Great Smoky Mountains. Peaks that at one time may have reached elevations of 10,000 to 12,000 feet are only half that size now. Rain, sleet, snow, and freezing and thawing over eons of time have shaped these mountains into the gentler Smokies we know today. The higher elevations during particularly wet cycles may receive as much as a hundred inches of precipitation in a single year, which ultimately translates into the picturesque streams and waterfalls we have all come to associate with the Smokies. Who isn't captivated by the rush of water weaving its way around the emerald green, moss-covered boulders of Roaring Fork?

Foreword

by Bill Lea

Water truly is the life-blood of the Smokies. The abundant precipitation that falls upon these mountains creates the lush plant life so characteristic of this temperate rain forest. A vast array of wildflowers display their colors throughout the growing season. People from across the country are drawn to the annual Smoky Mountains Spring Wildflower Pilgrimage. The combination of elevation changes, plentiful moisture, and rich soils give rise to more than a hundred different tree species. In fact, there is a greater diversity of trees in the half-million acres of the Smokies than all of Europe!

When visitors come to the Great Smoky Mountains, the animal they most hope to see is the black bear. Fairy tales and media sensationalism have created an image of an animal that few people understand, but one that nearly everyone hopes to see. These powerful but shy mammals deserve our respect. Observing a black bear from a safe distance may be the highlight of a person's visit to the Smokies. But don't forget about the other critters such as white-tailed deer, elk, raccoons, songbirds, butterflies, and even salamanders.

When I think of the Smokies, I picture her mystic mountain moods most often. I have been atop Clingmans Dome enjoying distant views only to be swallowed up in the clouds a moment later. Following a spring thunderstorm I may be mesmerized by the beauty of a rising mist as the sun breaks through a dramatic sky. Weather and scenes can change in a heartbeat, giving personality and moods to the mountains here.

I would like to thank Jerry Greer and Nye Simmons, my collaborators on this project, for giving me the opportunity to express in this introduction how we all feel about the Smokies. I know that we want nothing more than to be ready, with camera in hand, to catch the wonder and light of these Great Smoky Mountains!

Above: A white-tailed deer forages in the morning mist of Cades Cove (Bill Lea).

Right: Evening mist is bathed in sunset light at Morton Overlook, high on the Smokies' crest (Jerry Greer).

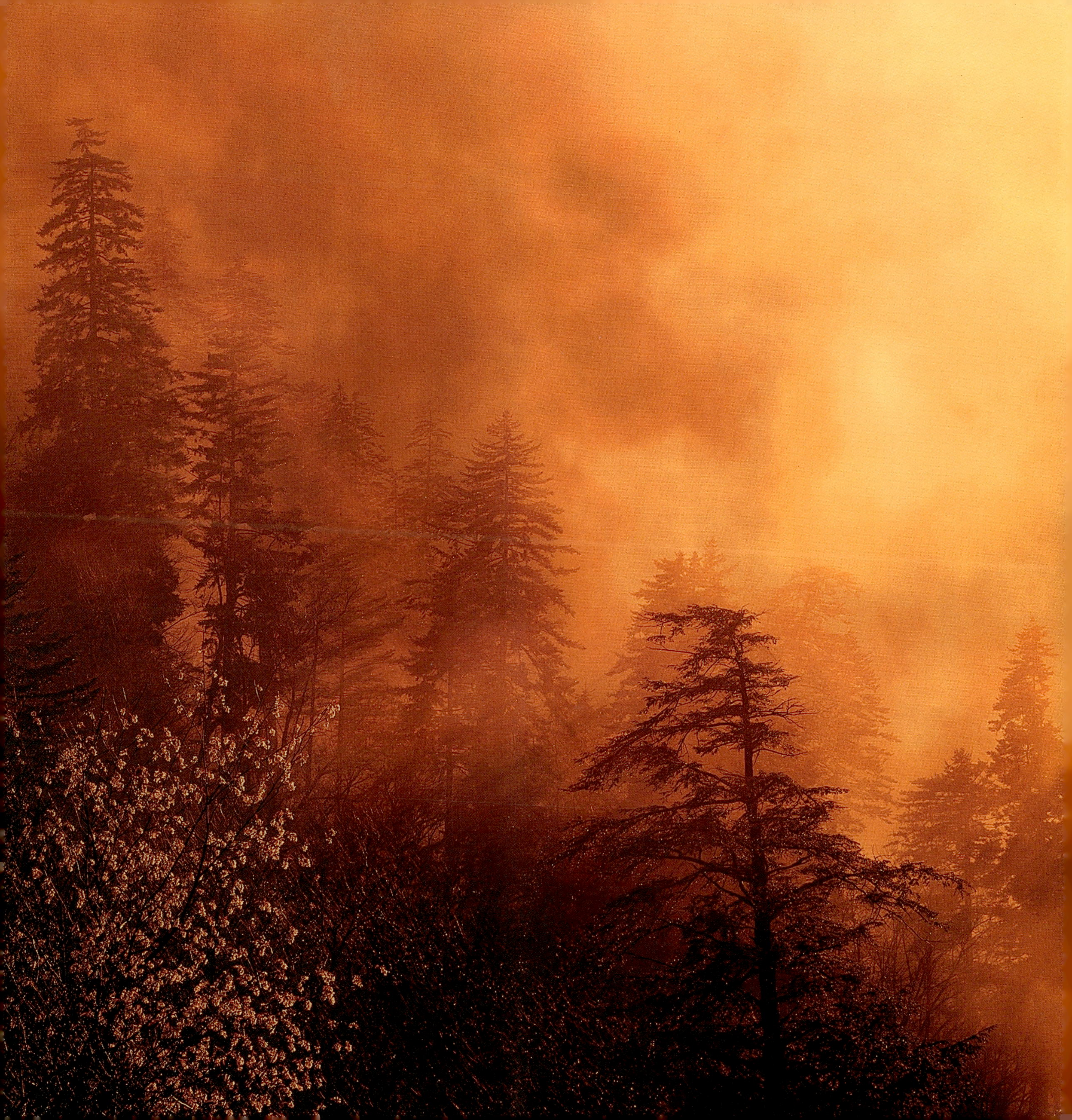

Above: Late light graces a snowy landscape high in the Smokies (Bill Lea).

Right: Ice clinging to rock and plants creates a winter fantasy (Nye Simmons).

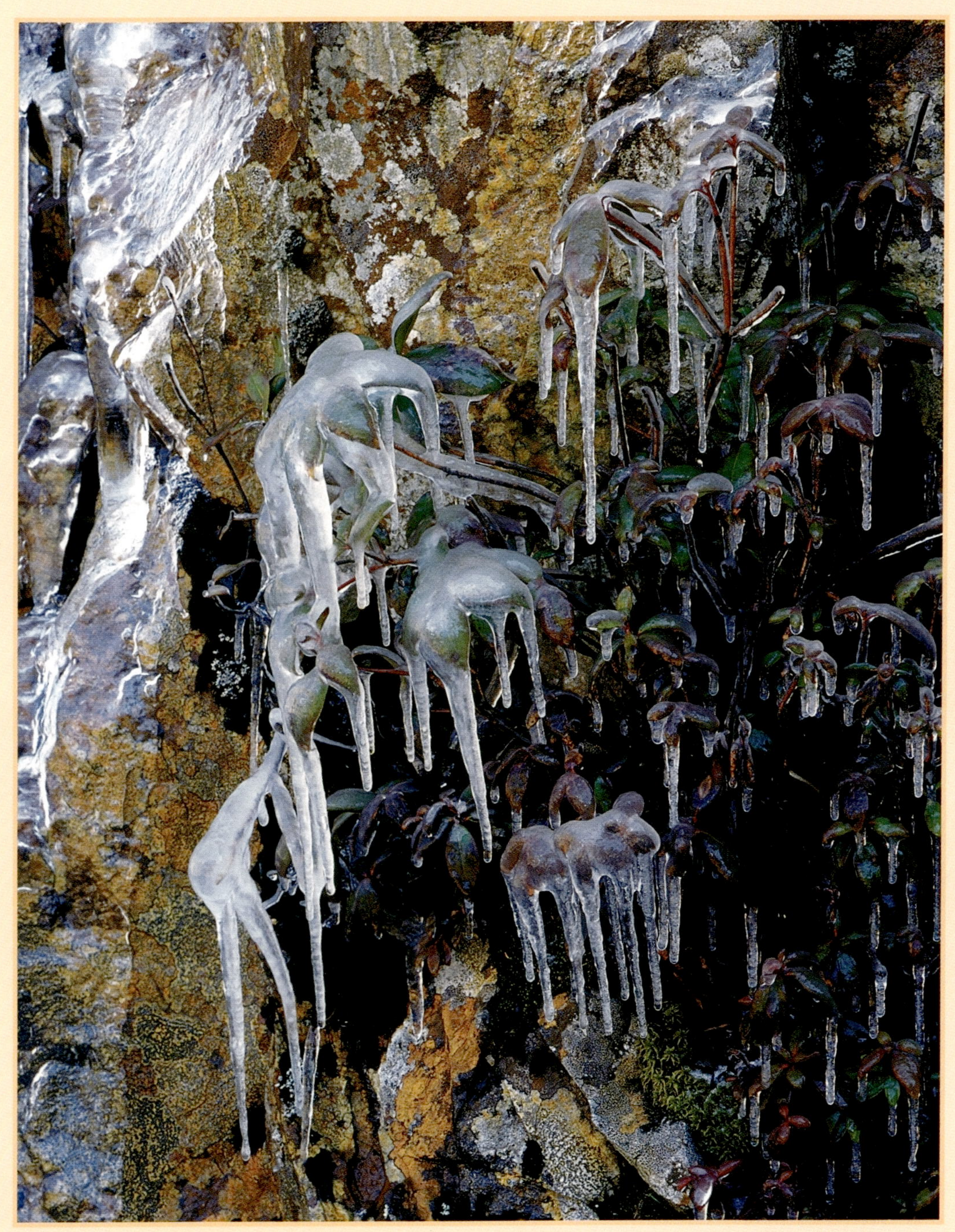

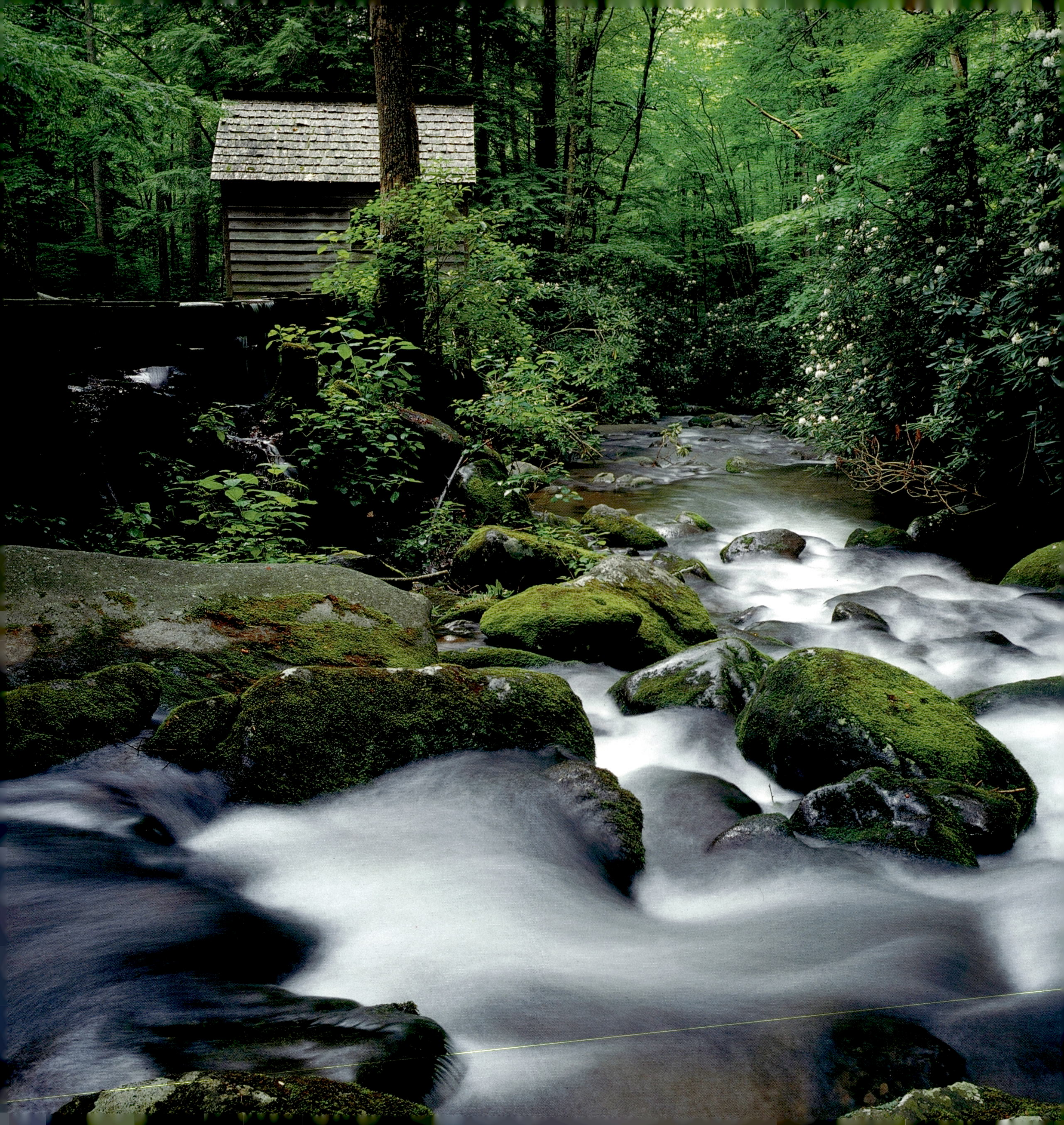

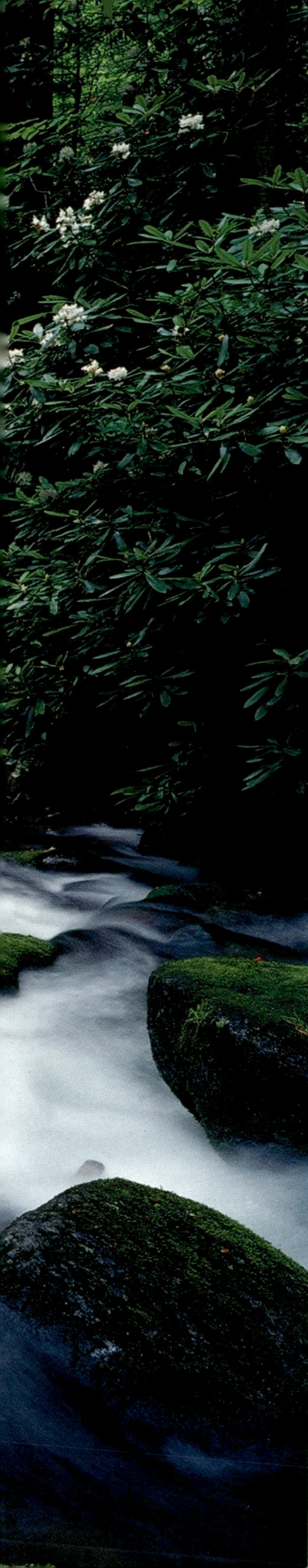

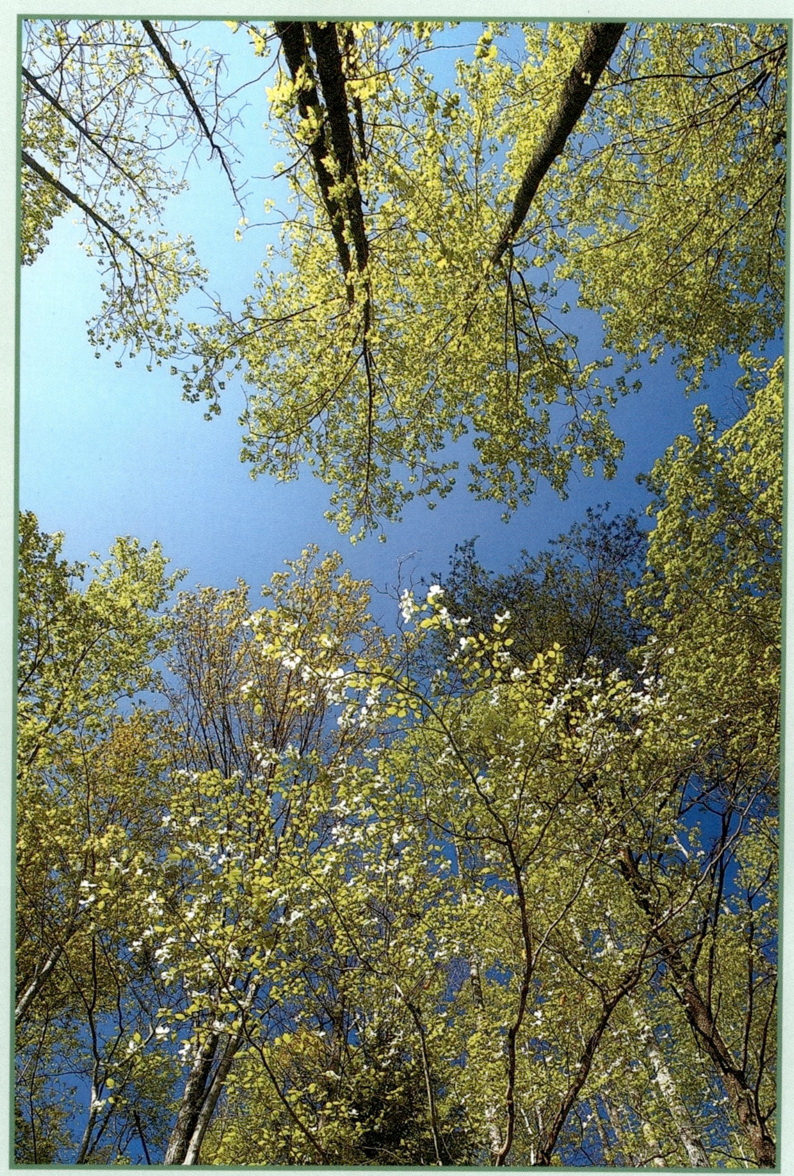

ALFRED REAGAN PLACE, stop #12 on the Roaring Fork Motor Nature Trail, was built by Alfred Regan, who was a prosperous farmer and jack-of-all trades of the Roaring Fork community. Many such historic buildings are found throughout the Park (Nye Simmons).

Above: Spring comes to the Smokies (Jerry Greer).

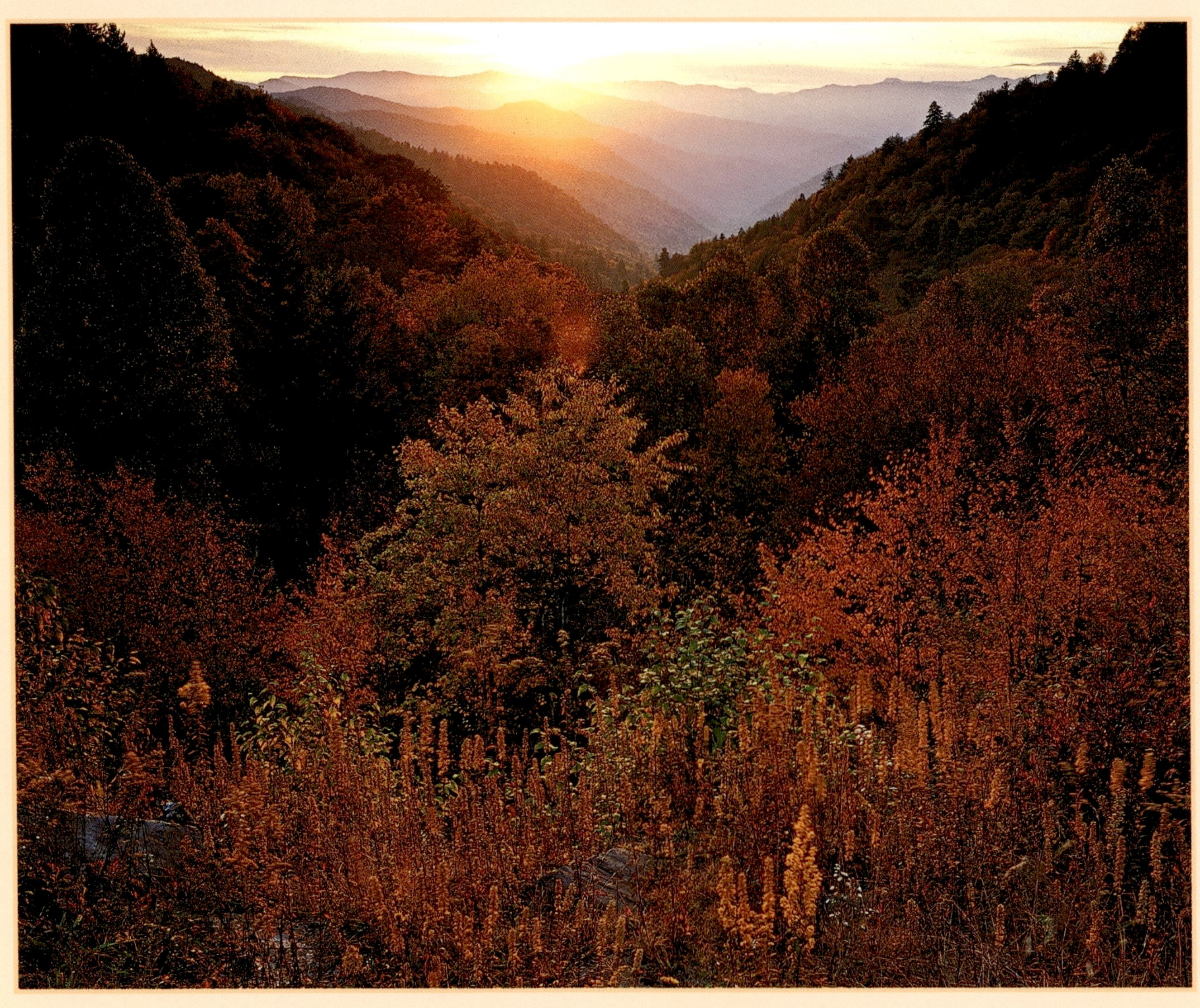

Above: An autumn sunrise view from the Oconoluftee Overlook (Nye Simmons).

Right: Raccoons are among the Smokies' most curious wild denizens (Bill Lea).

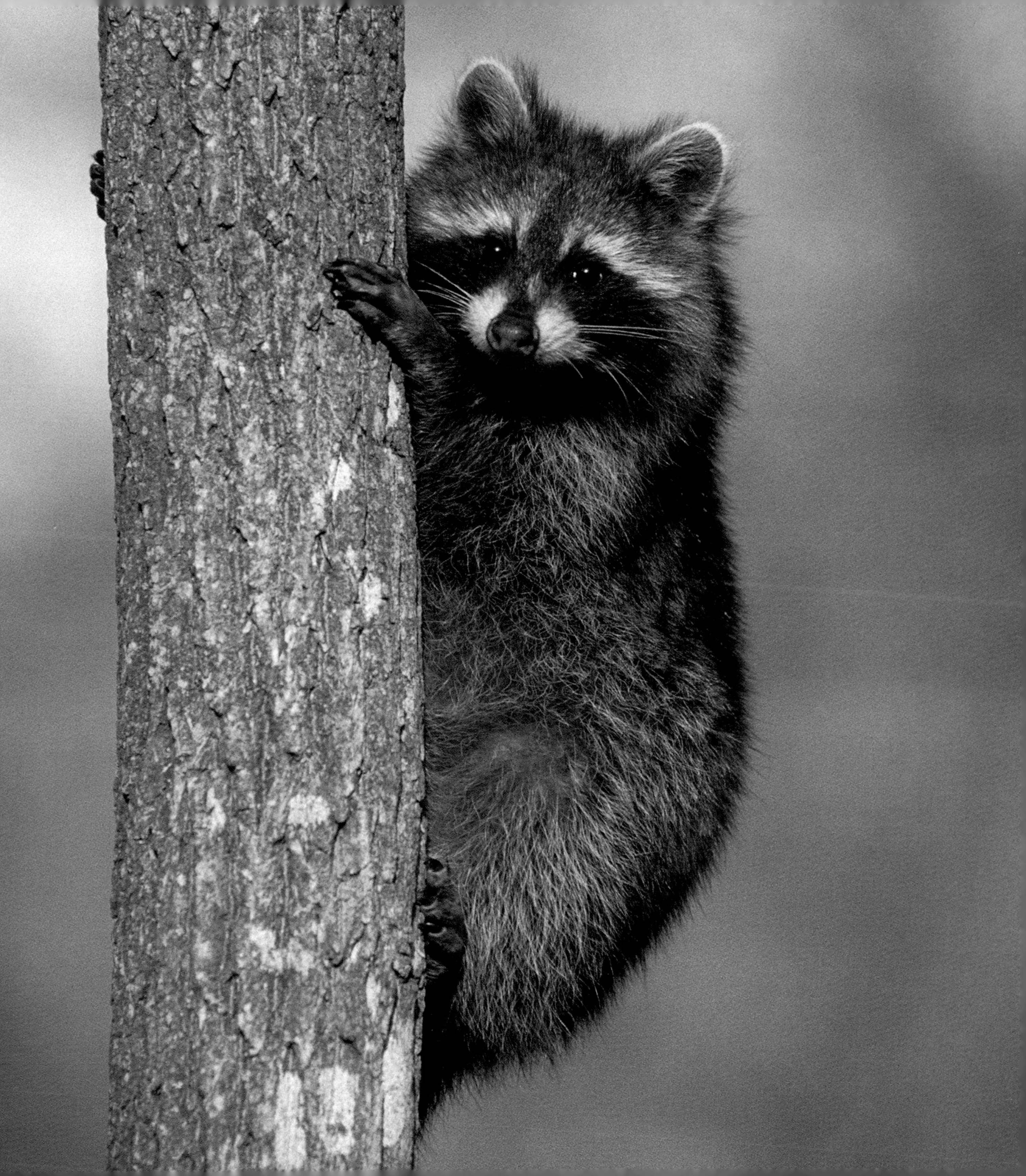

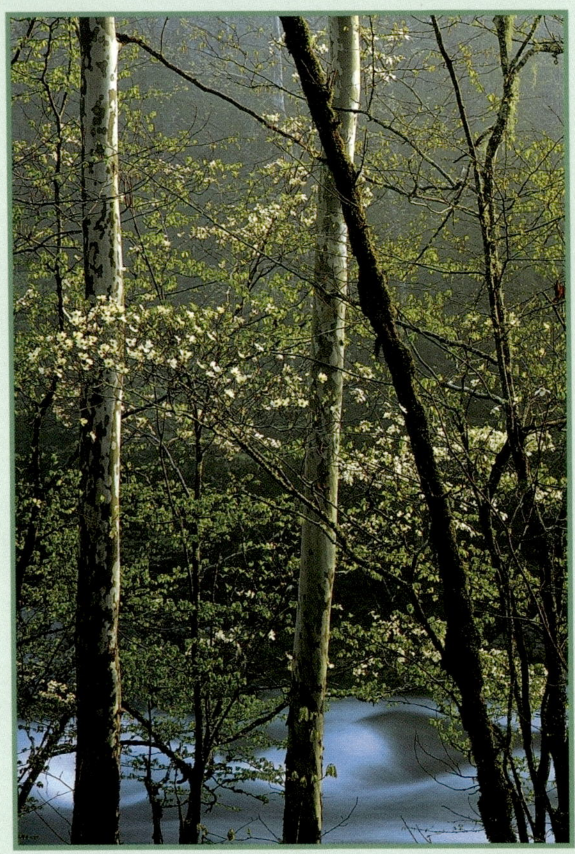

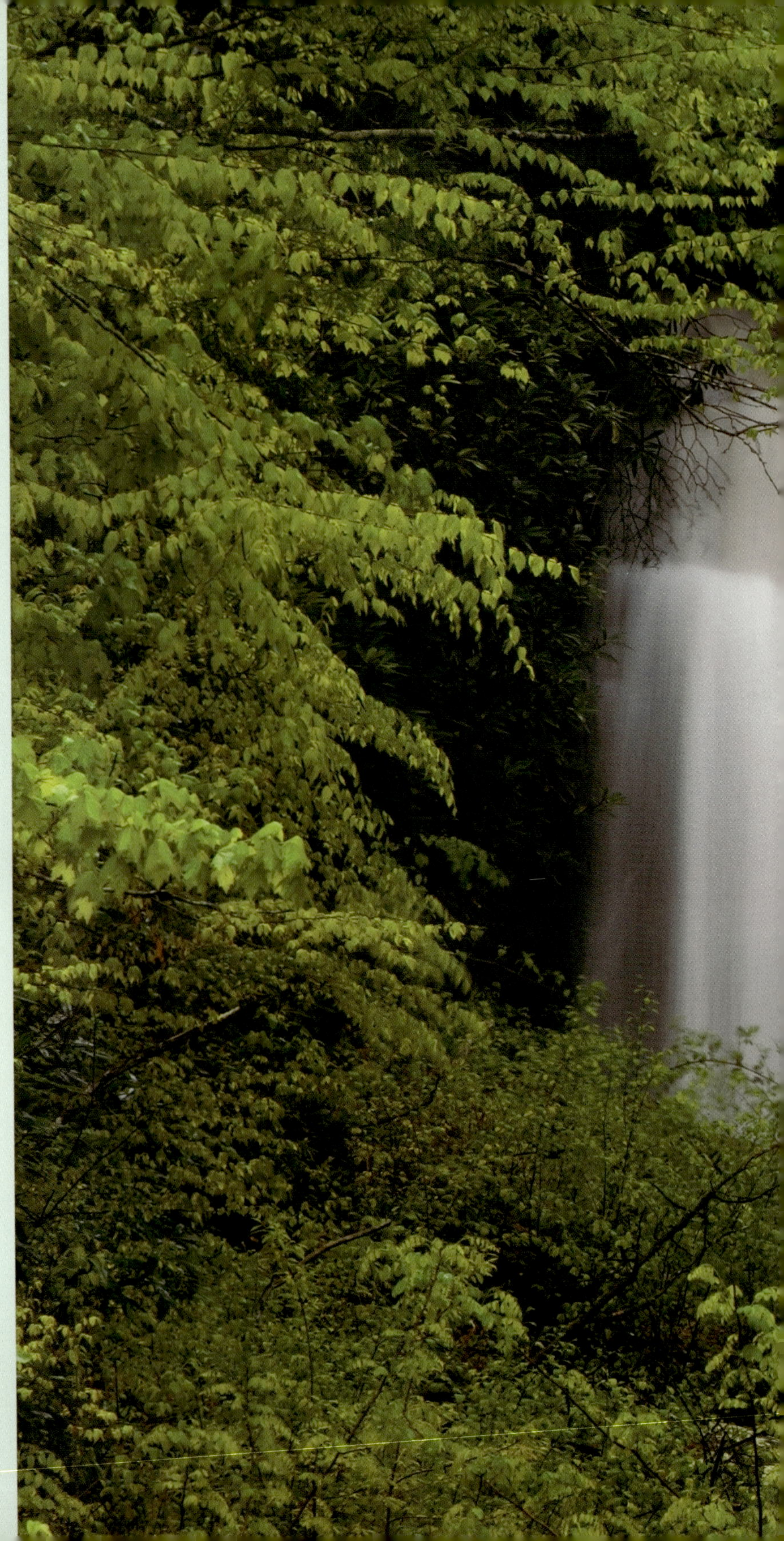

Above: Dogwood trees bloom in spring along the Little Pigeon River, located in Greenbrier (Jerry Greer).

Right: Spring greens surround Meigs Falls (Bill Lea).

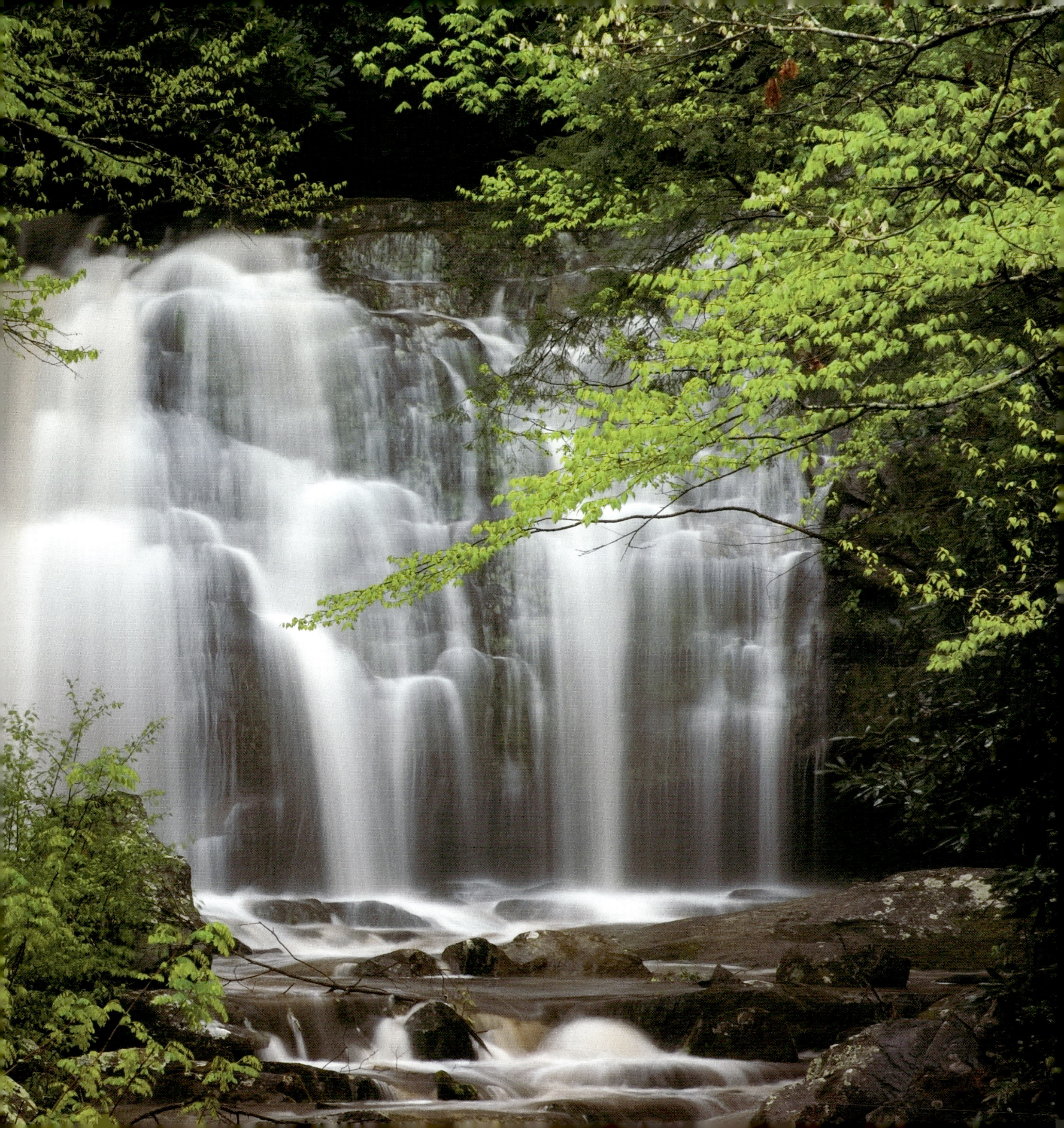

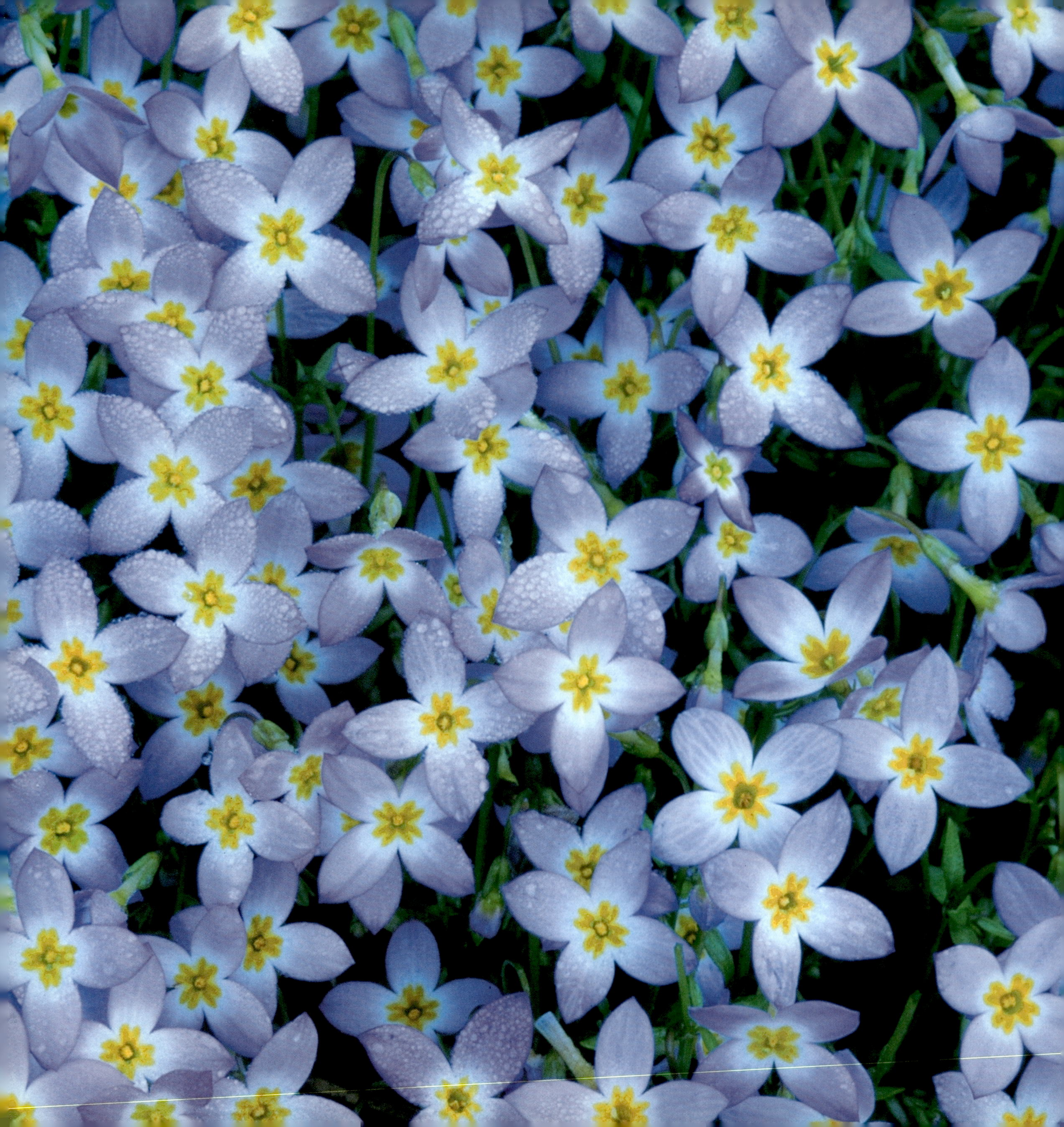

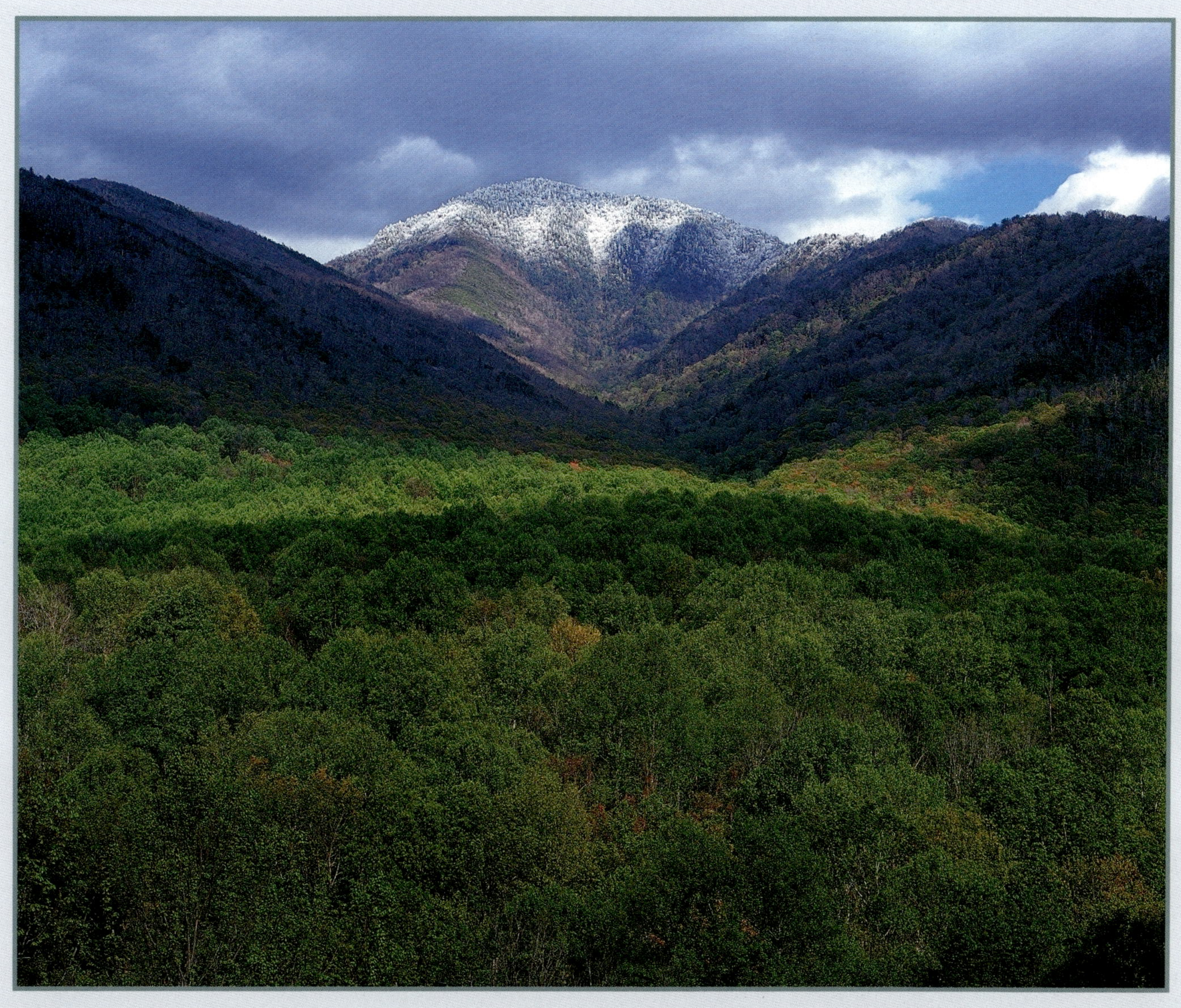

Left: A carpet of bluets covers the forest floor (Bill Lea).

Above: A spring snowstorm covers the high elevations of Mount Le Conte (Nye Simmons).

Next page: Tipton Place, located in Cades Cove, is one of the Smokies' most famous historic landmarks (Jerry Greer).

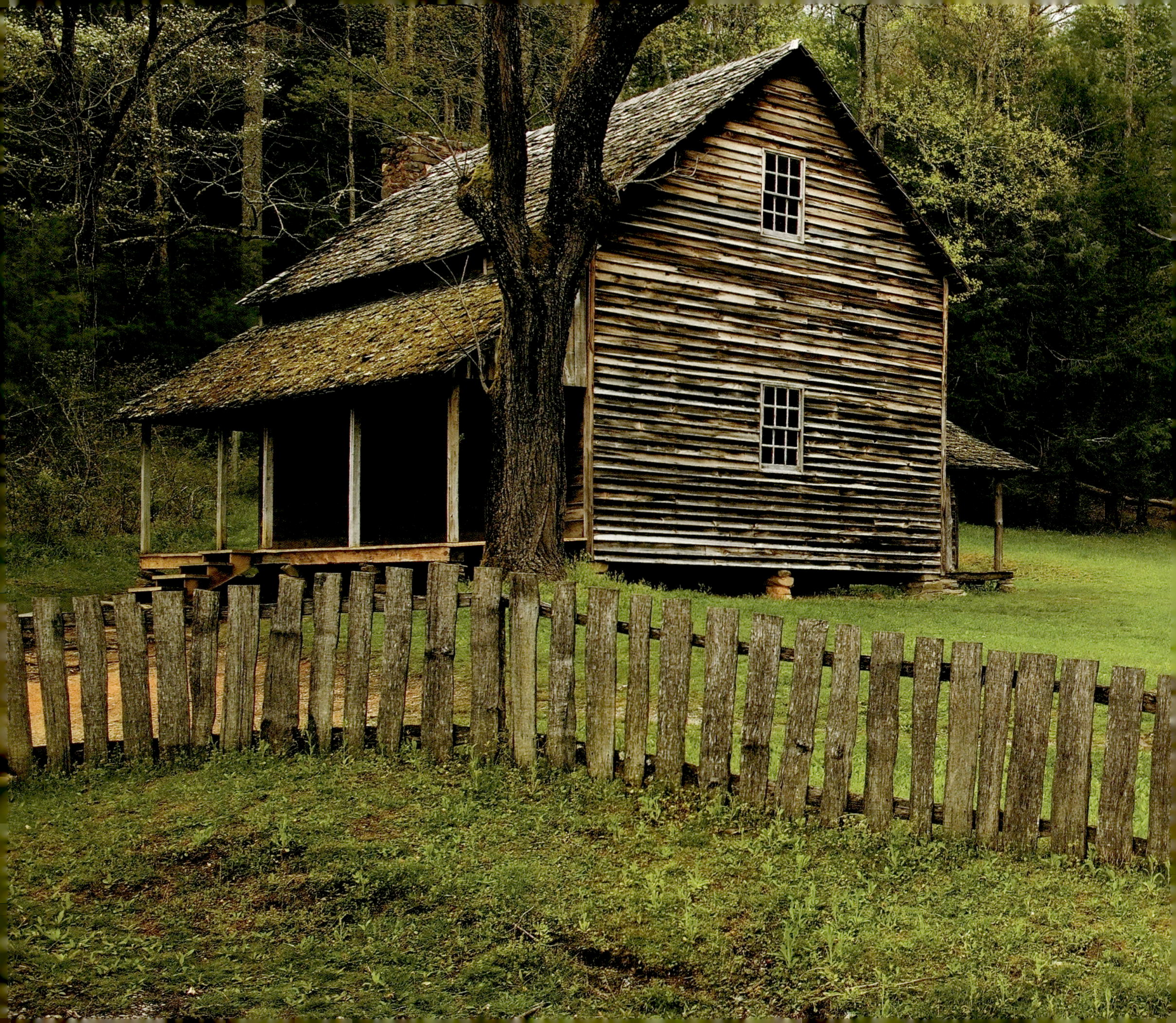

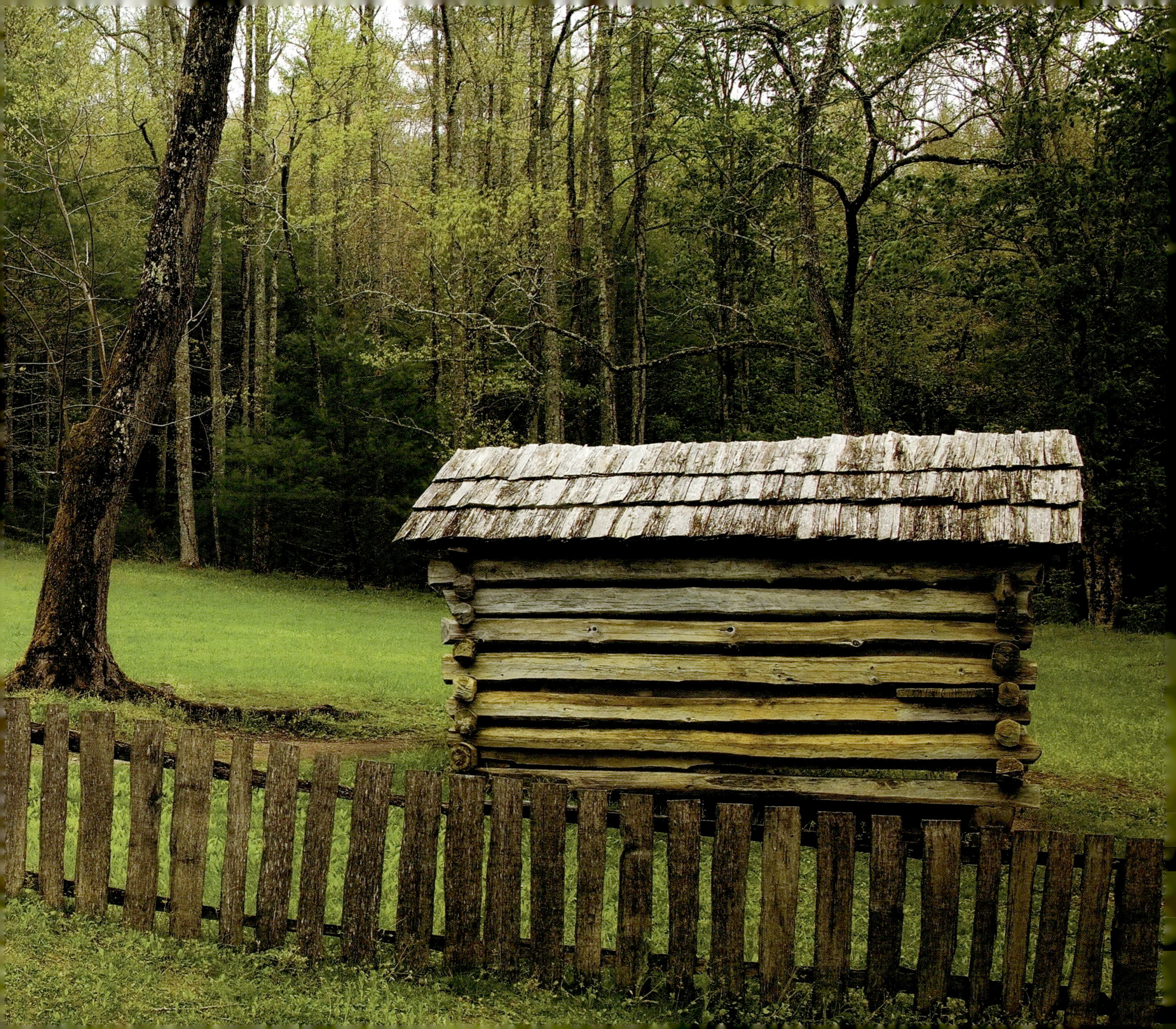

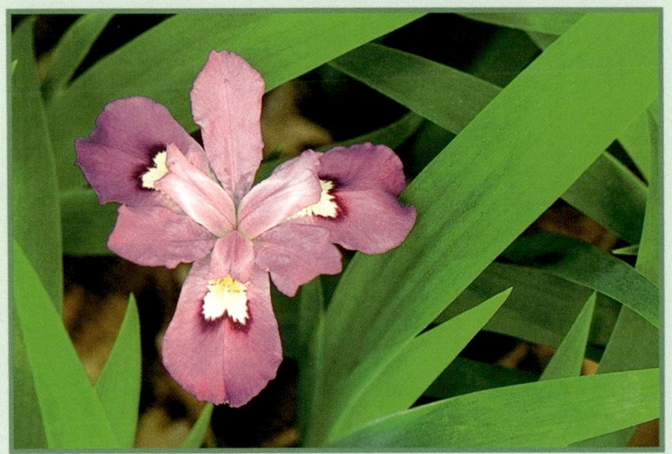

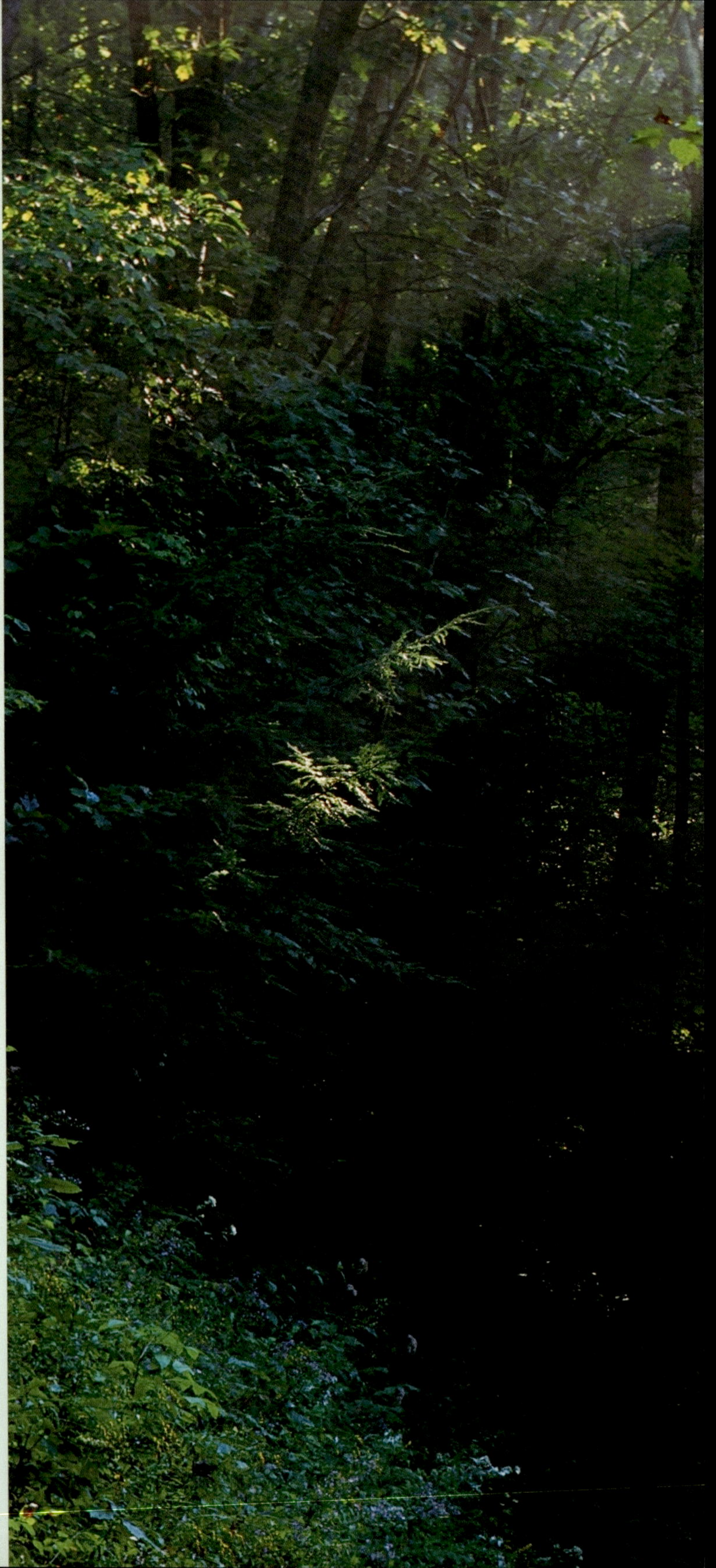

Above: Crested-dwarf iris (Bill Lea).

Right: Rays of sunlight penetrate the primordial forest (Bill Lea).

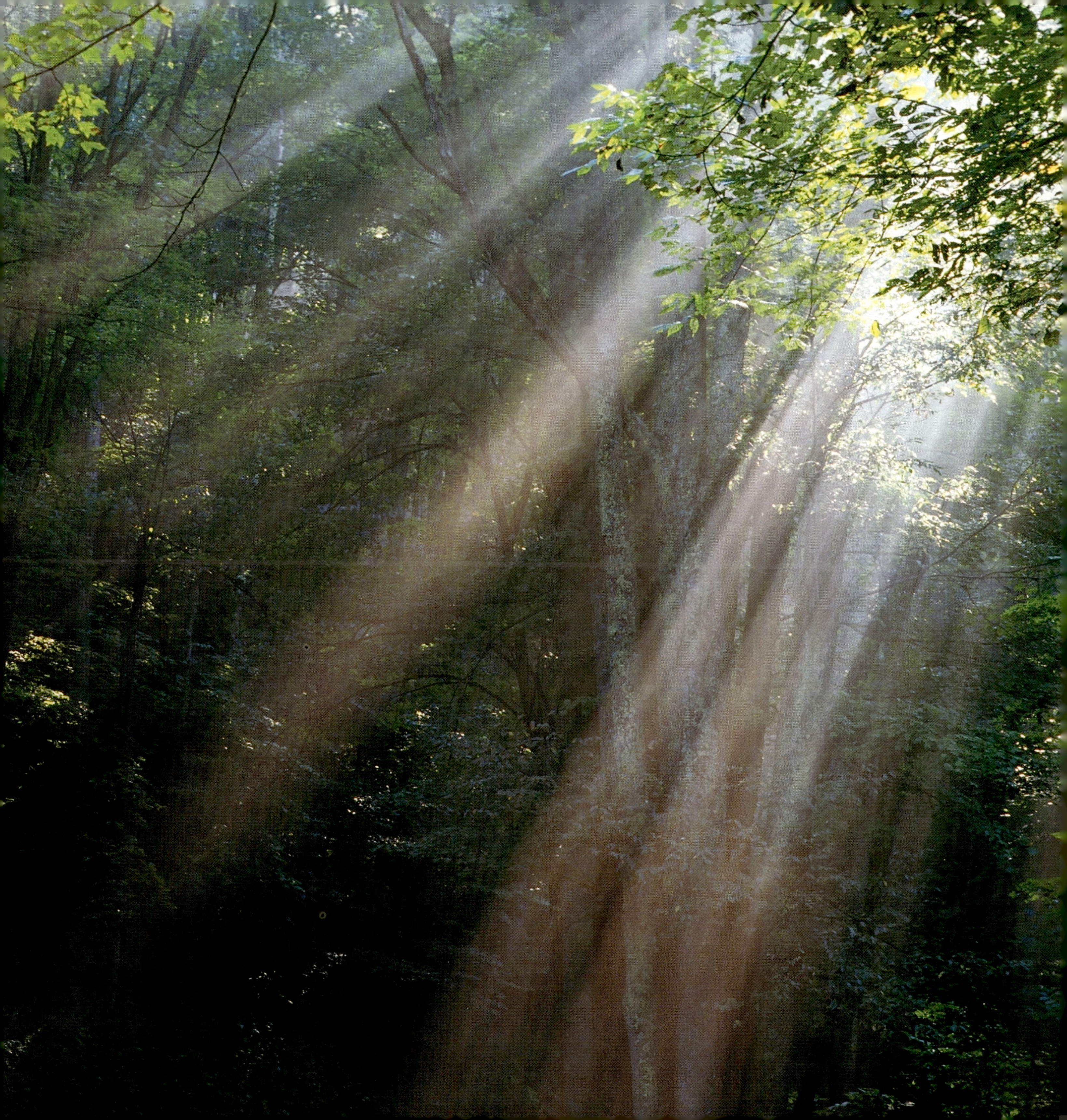

Above: Morning fog as seen from Myrtle Point on the slopes of Mount Le Conte (Jerry Greer).

Right: Twilight descends over an oak tree in Cades Cove (Bill Lea).

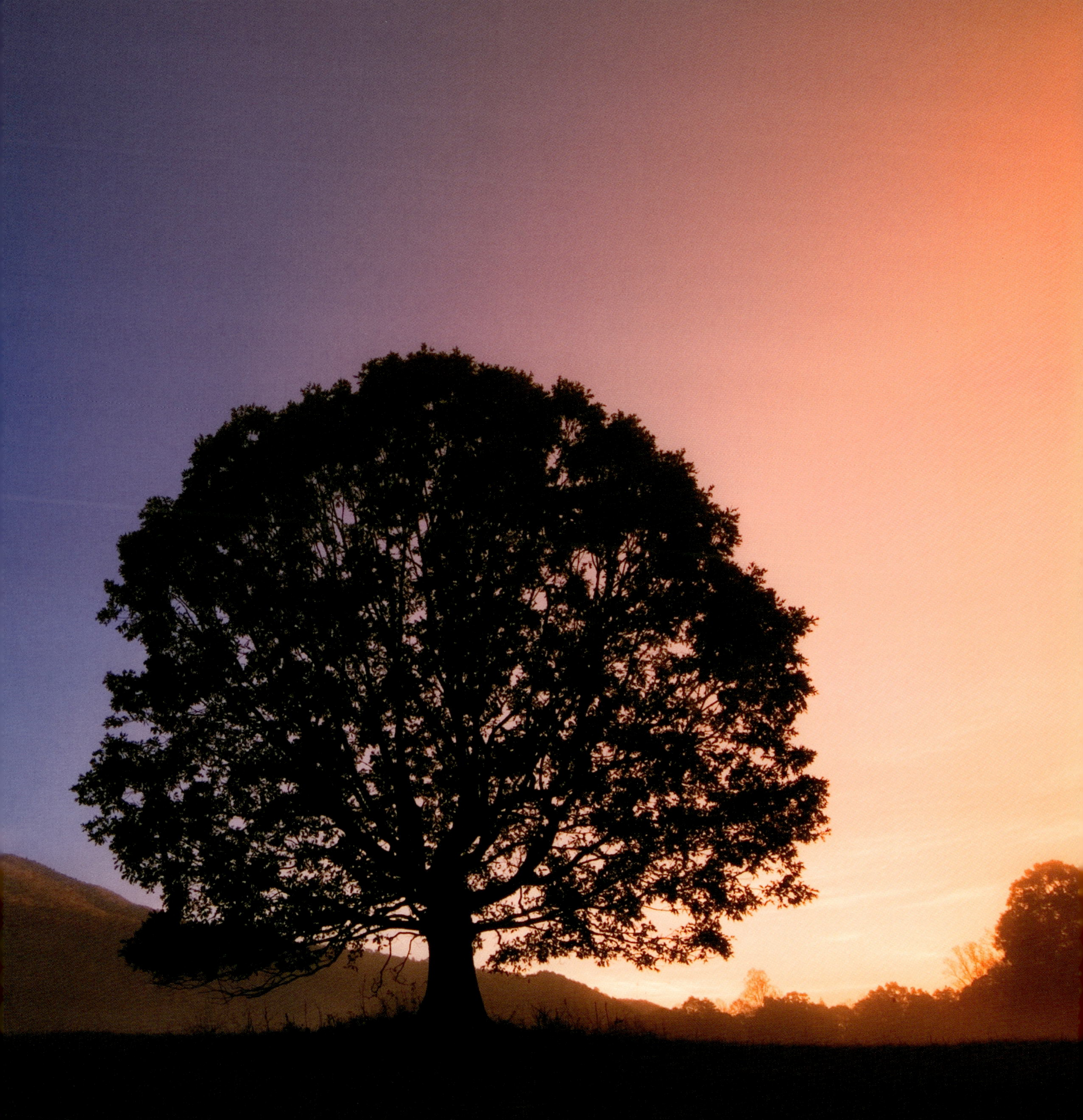

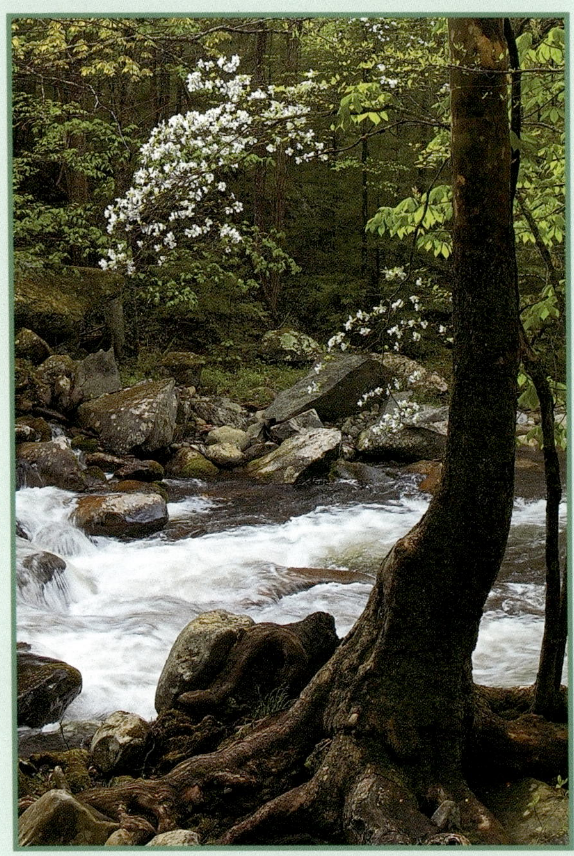

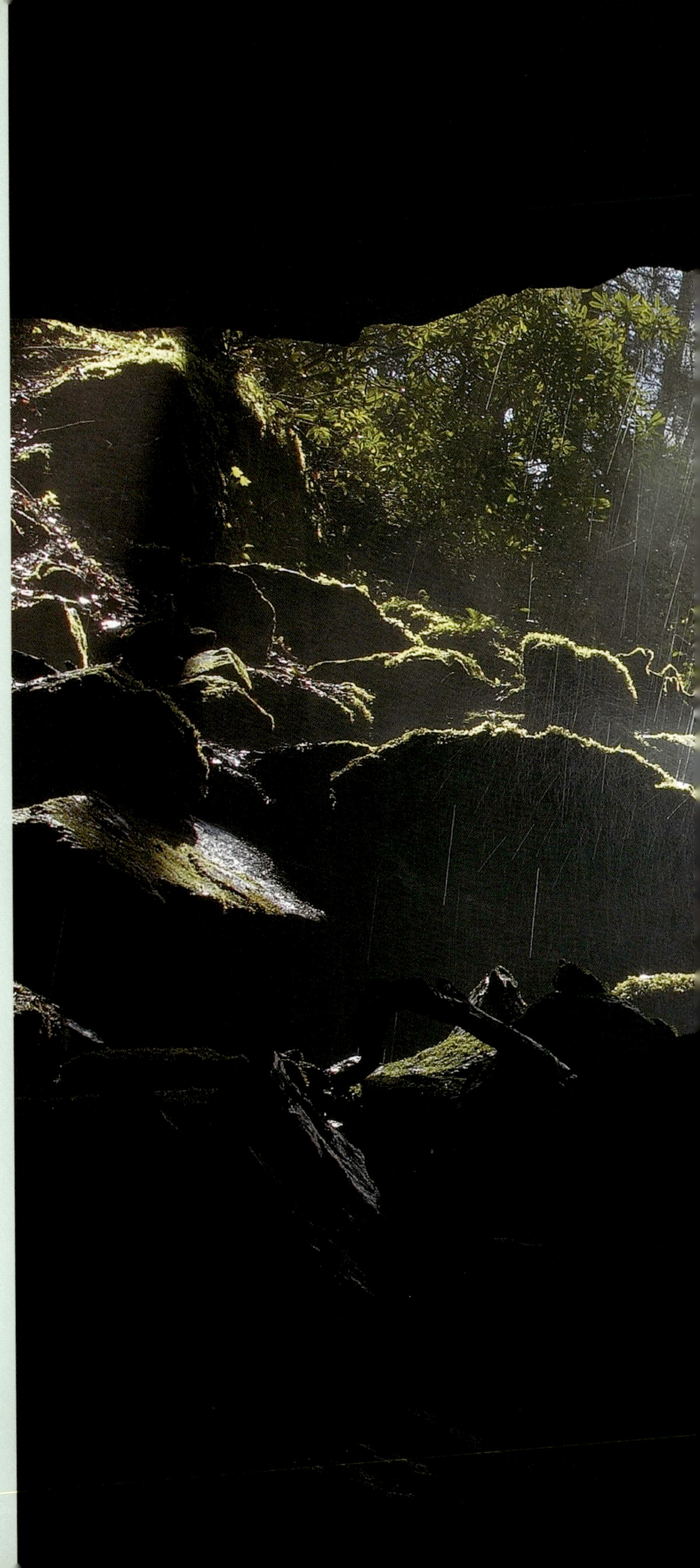

THE WHITE OAK SINK area of the Smokies is a natural limestone sink, and contains caves and waterfalls – or, as the case may be with White Oak Sink Falls, a cave behind a waterfall (Jerry Greer).

Above: Blooming dogwood and sycamore (Jerry Greer).

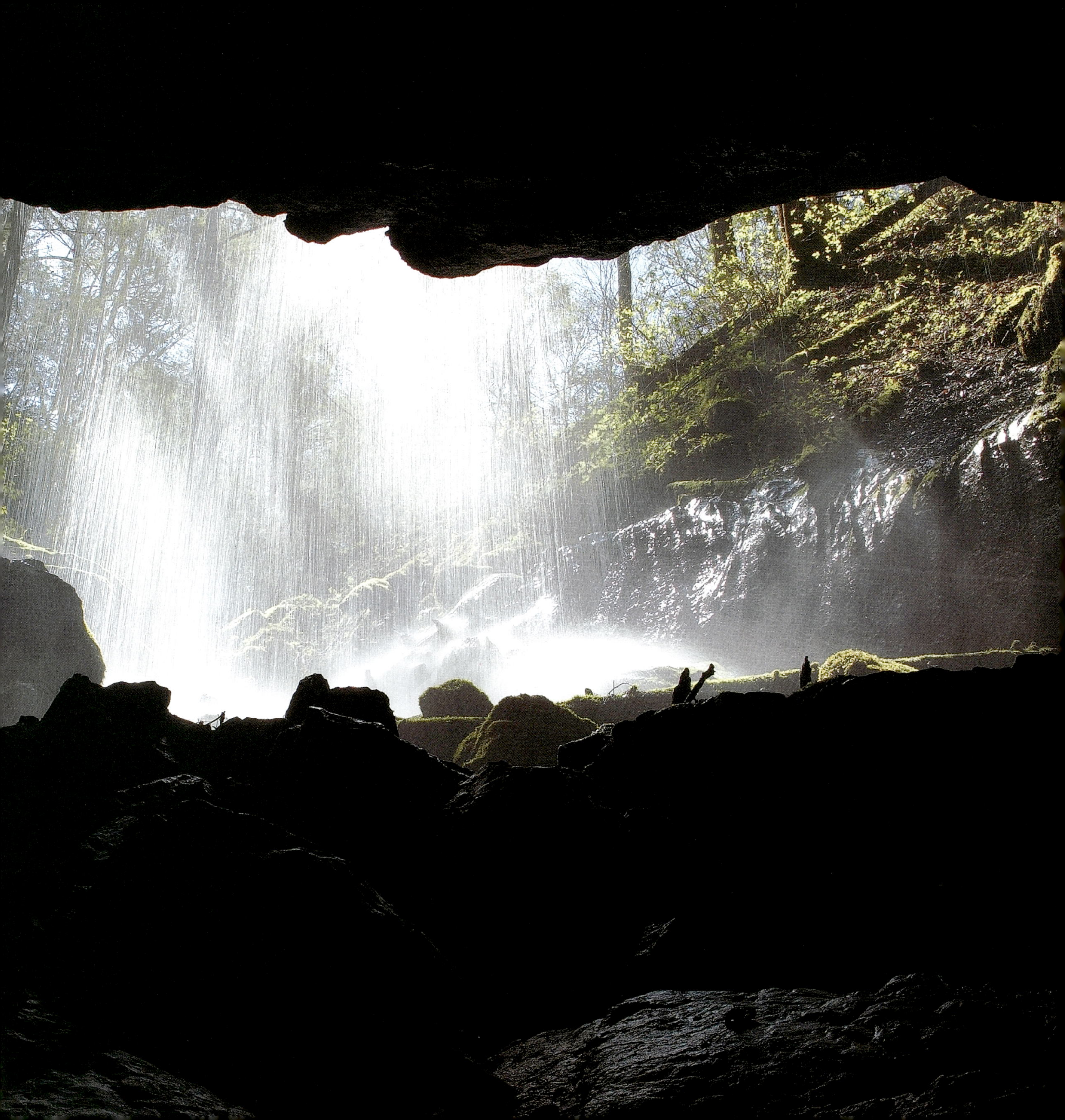

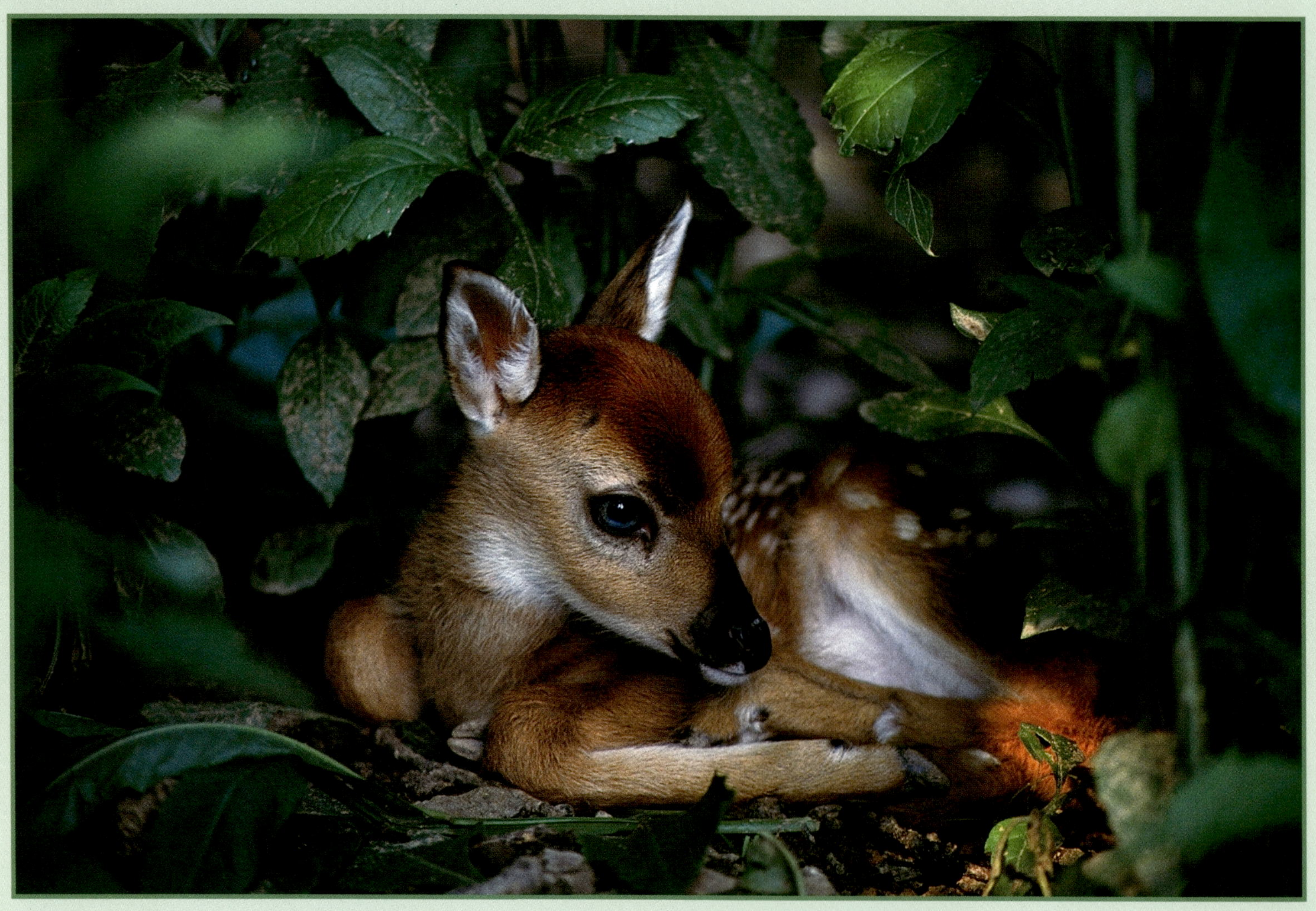

Above: A white-tailed deer fawn is trained by its mother to lie motionless whenever she is absent (Bill Lea).

Right: Place of a Thousand Drips Falls, located on the Roaring Fork Motor Nature Trail, is one of the Park's loveliest waterfalls (Nye Simmons).

Next page: Spring trees bud in White Oak Sink (Jerry Greer).

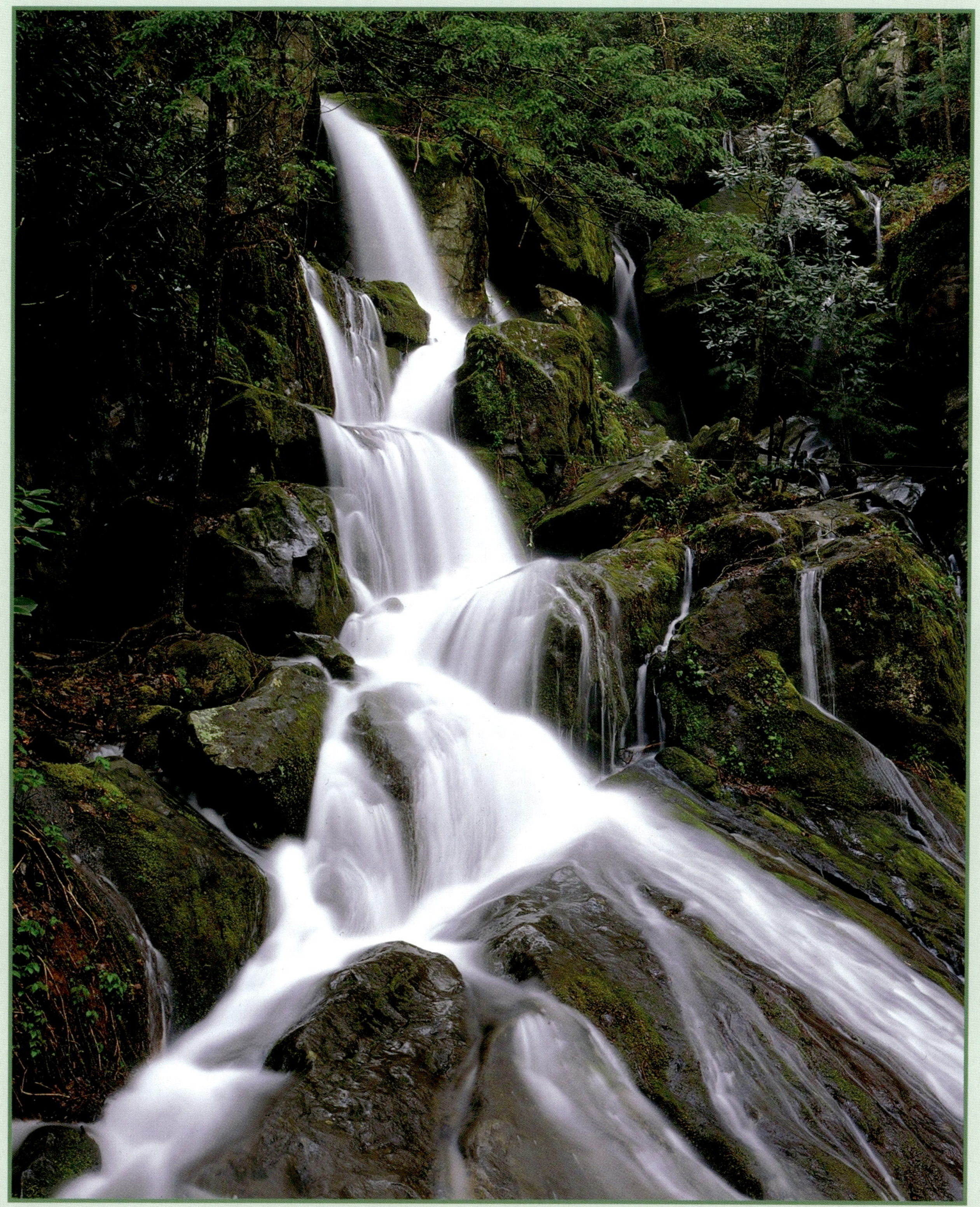

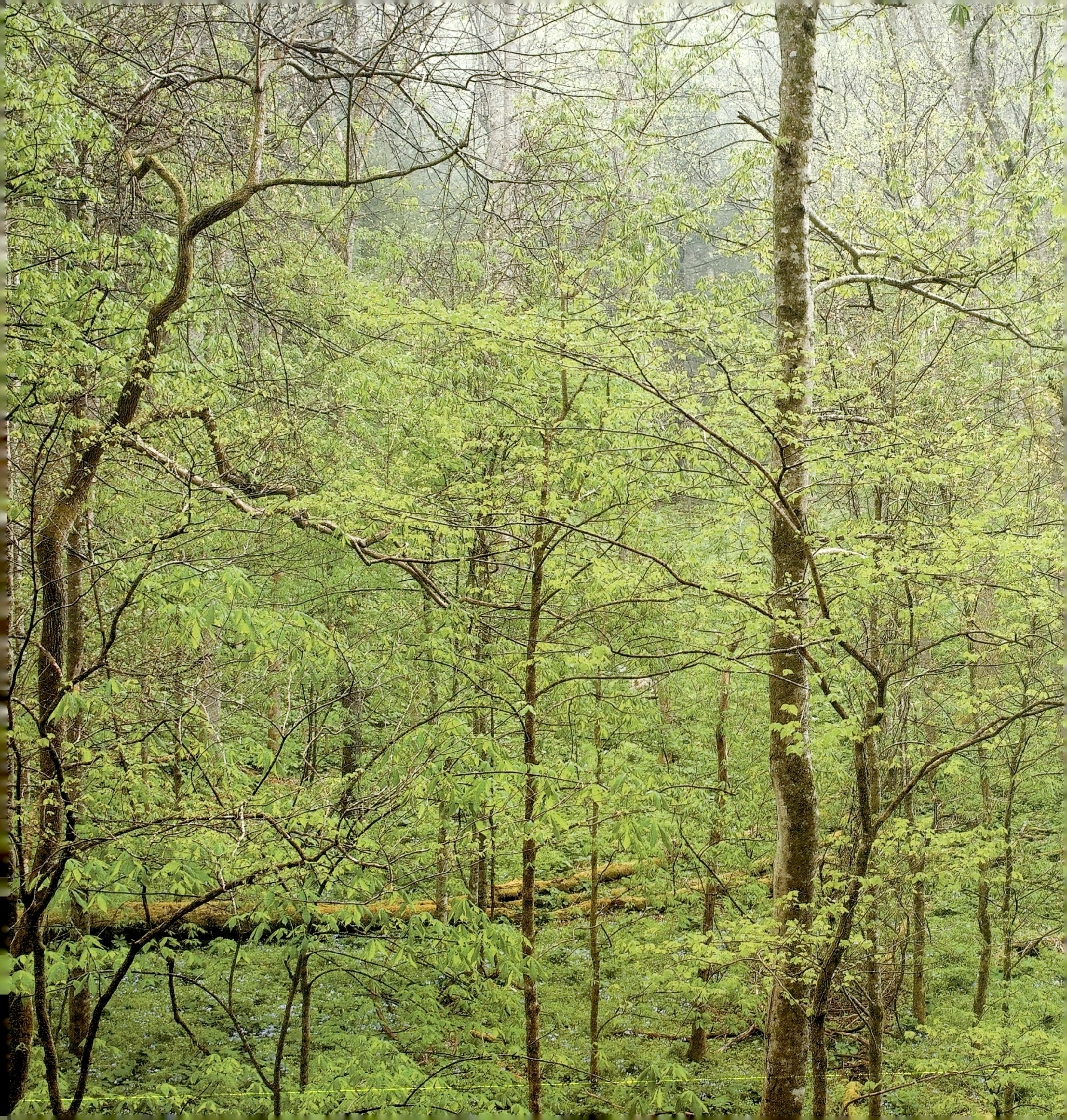

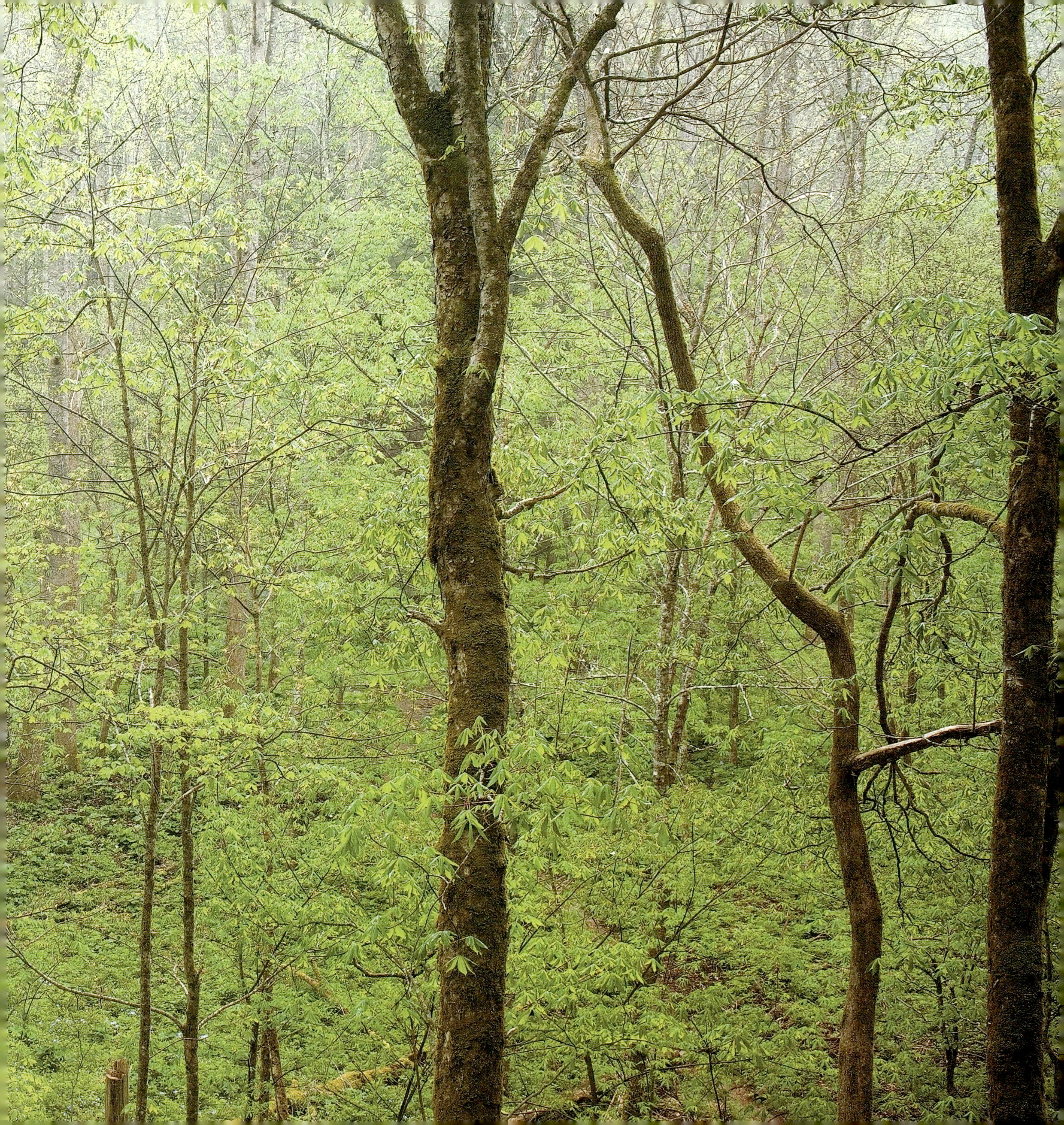

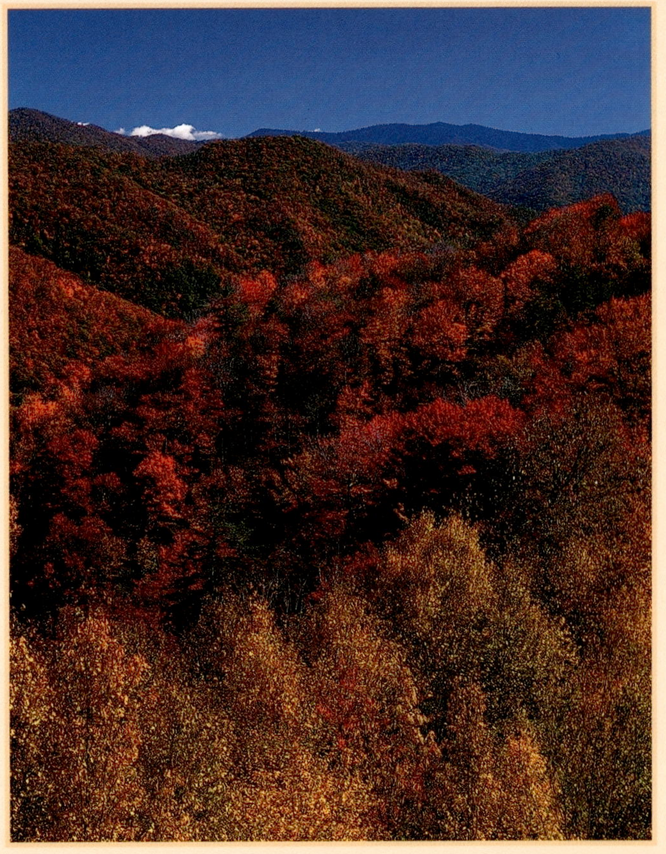

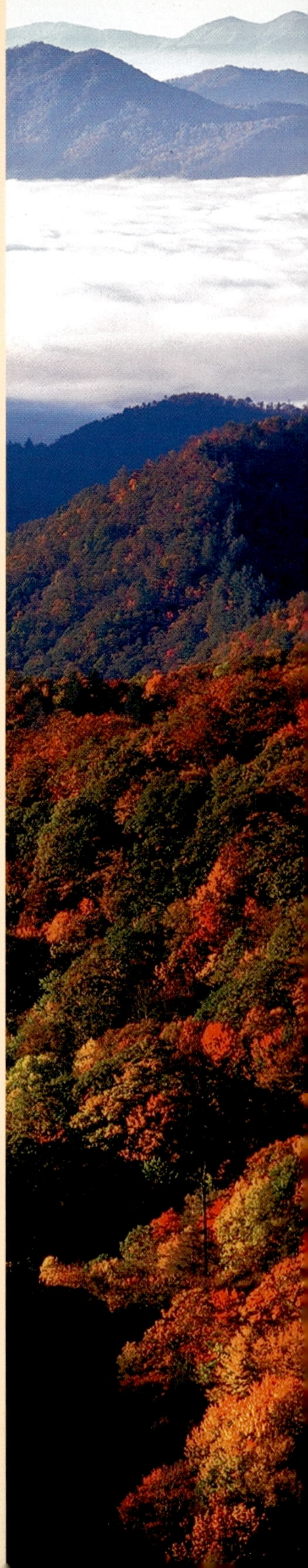

AUTUMN COMES to Shotbeech Ridge, overlooking morning fog on Lake Fontana. As elevations within the Park range from a few hundred feet above sea level to over 6000 feet, the Smokies have a diversity of trees found in few other places. As a result, fall foliage in the Smokies is spectacular (Nye Simmons).

Above: A line of maples blaze crimson in autumn (Nye Simmons).

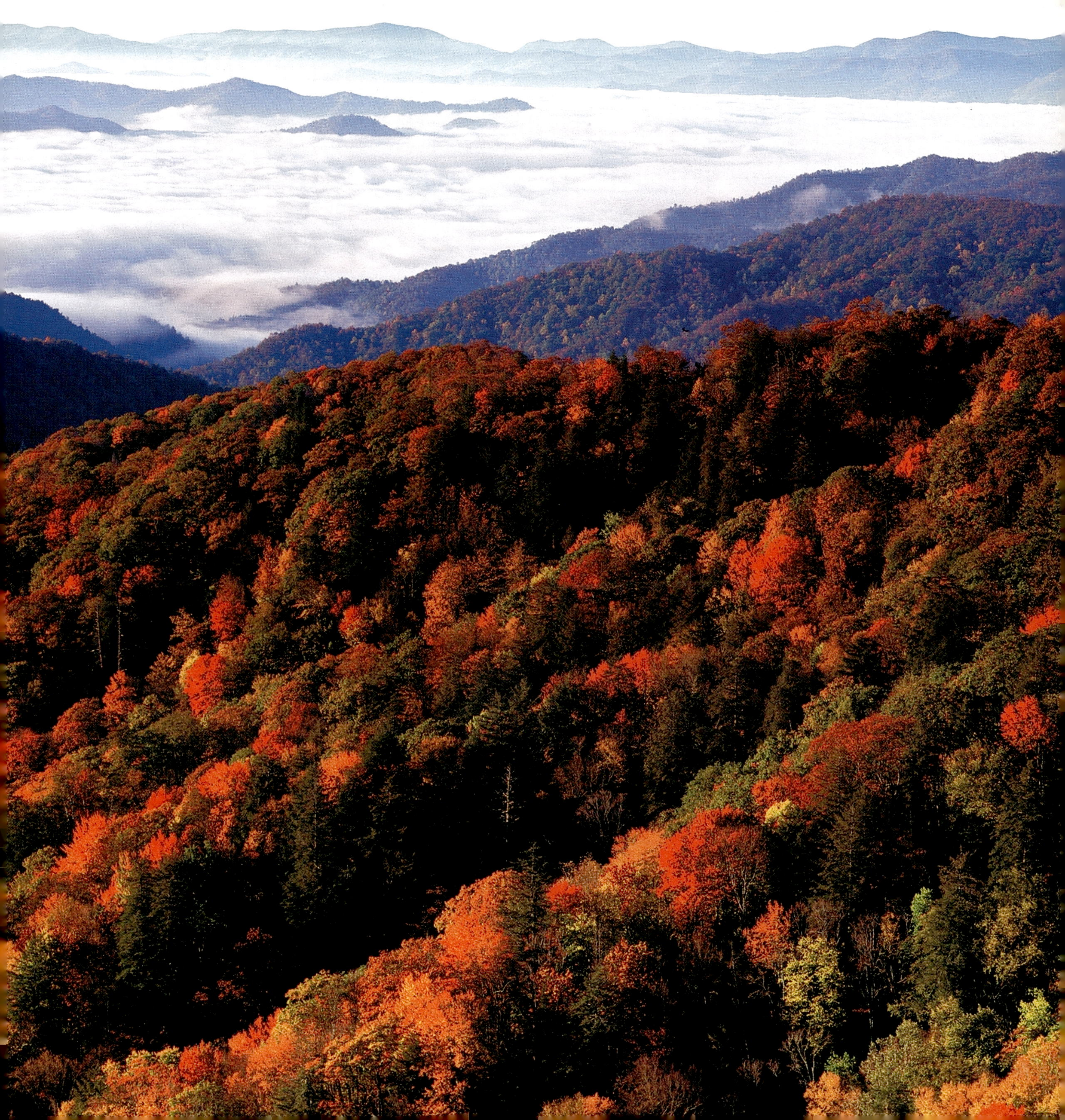

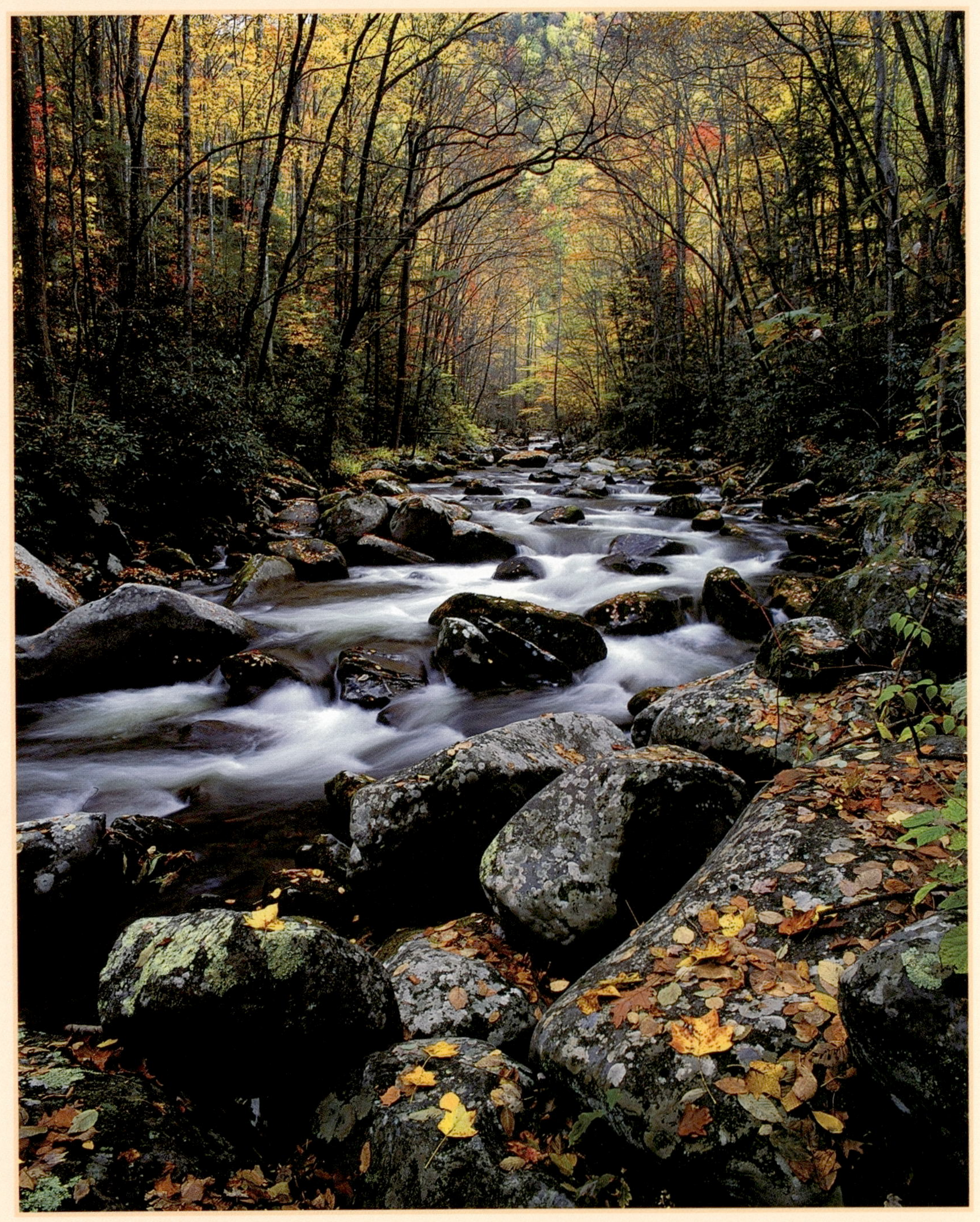

Above: Fall color along Big Creek (Nye Simmons).

Right: Pileated woodpeckers are an uncommon yet welcome sight in the Smokies (Bill Lea).

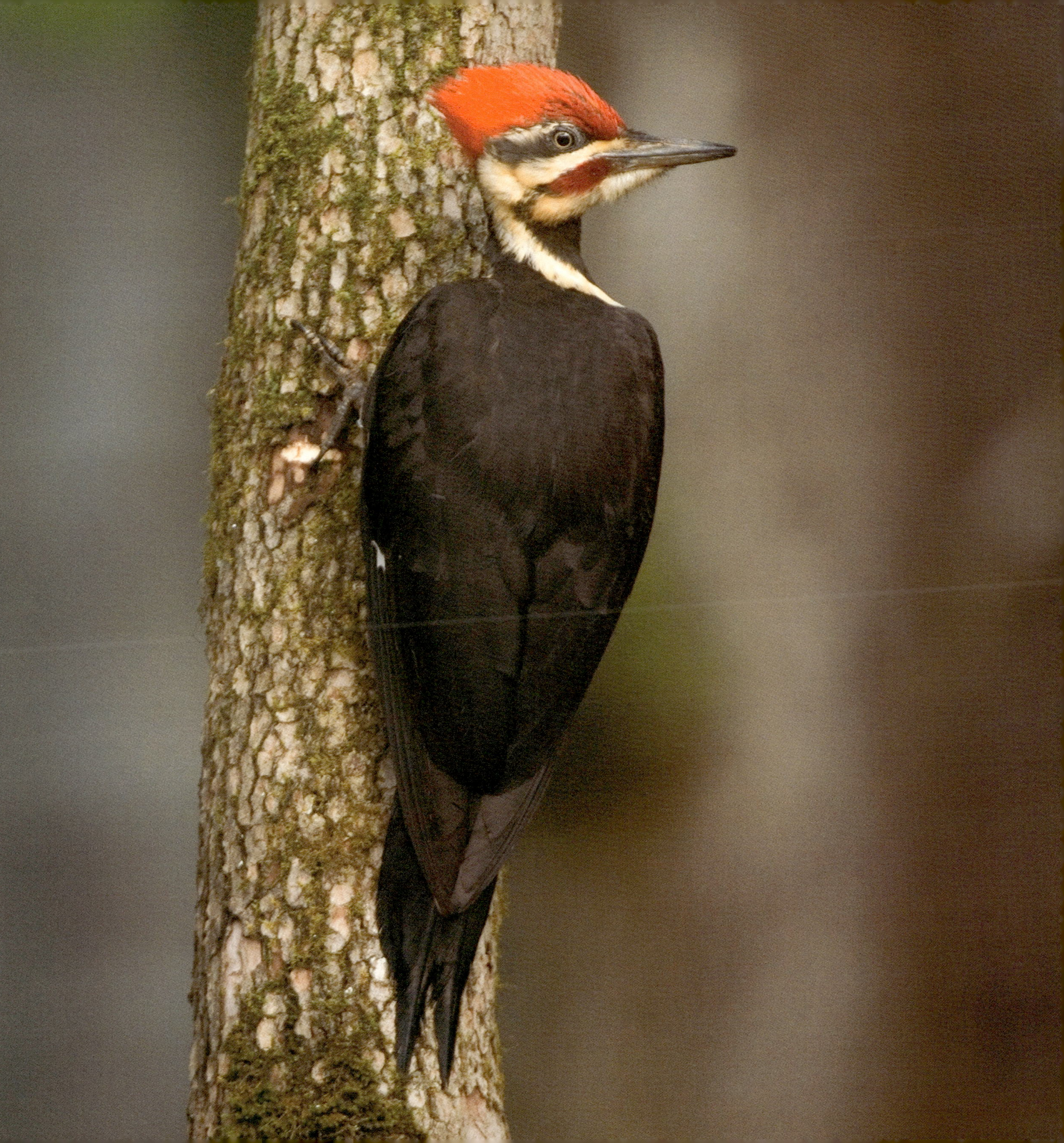

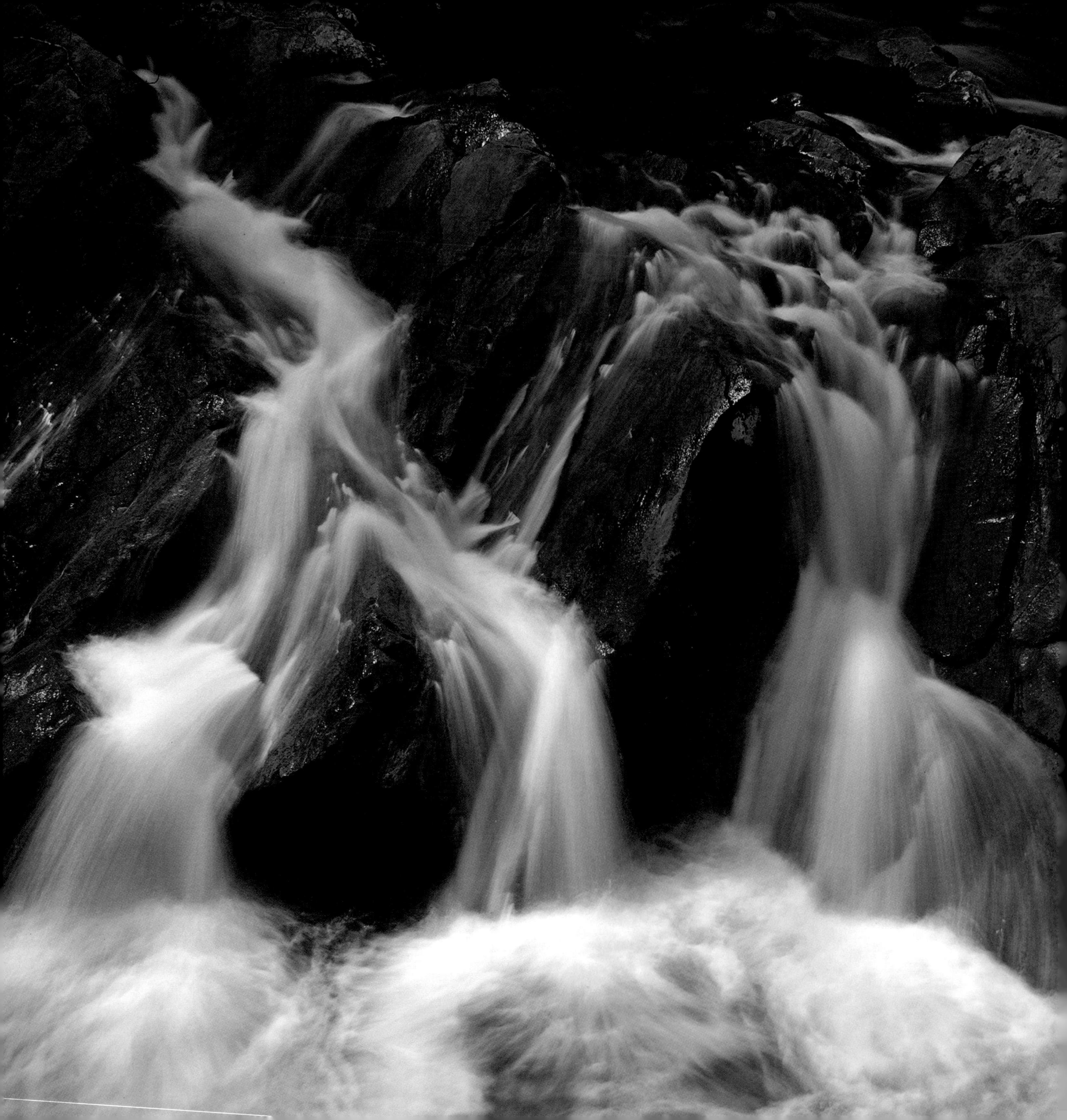

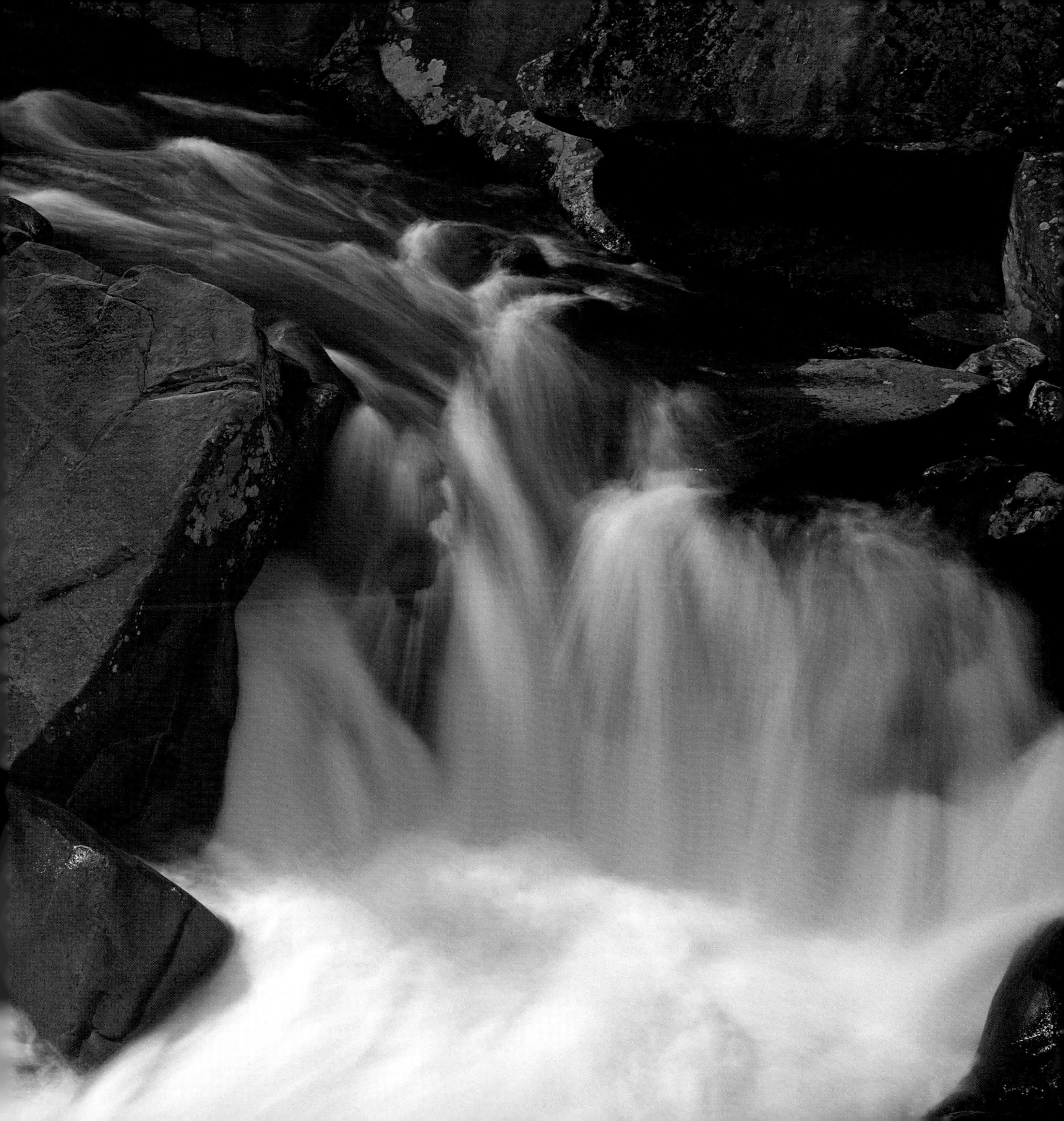

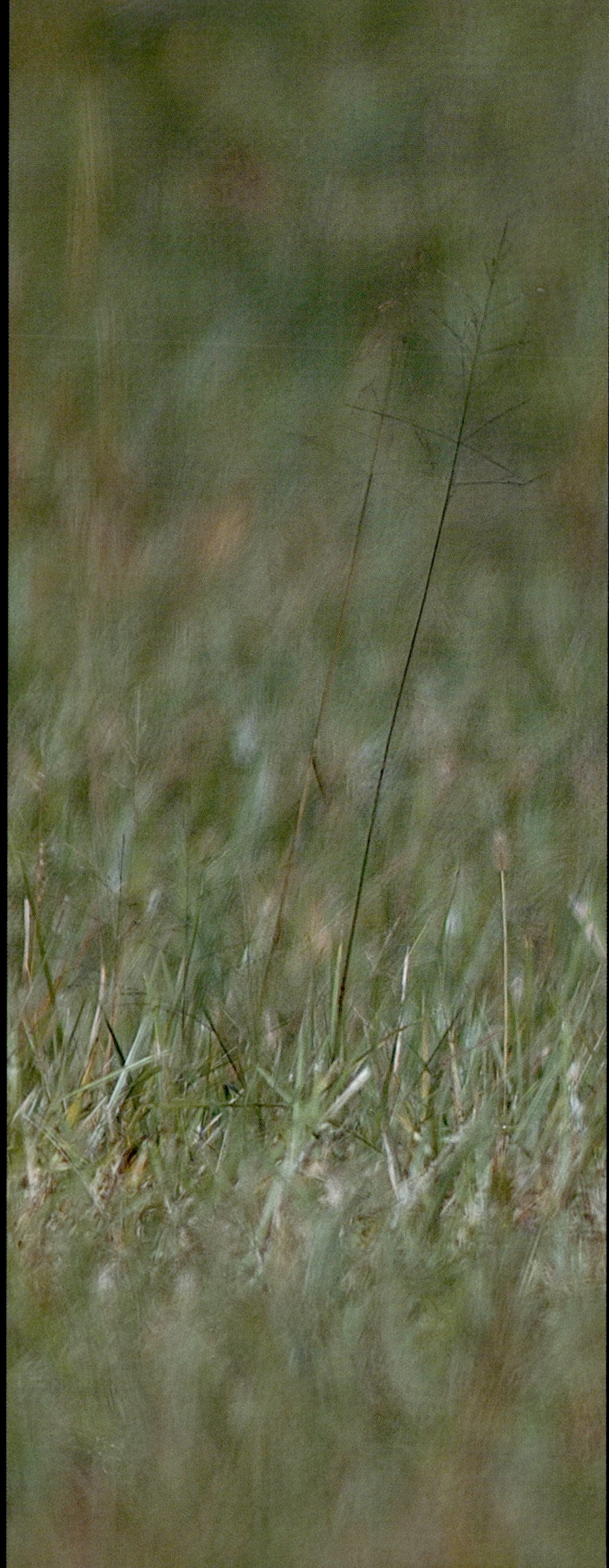

COYOTE ARE resourceful and intelligent animals, a fact that has allowed them to thrive even in areas of significant human activity. Coyote moved into the Smokies around 1985, and although their numbers are currently low, they appear to be increasing in all areas of the Park (Bill Lea).

Previous page: The Sinks, located on the Little River (Nye Simmons).

Next page: An autumn view of Cades Cove (Nye Simmons).

Following pages: Several views of black bears, the Park's most famous residents.

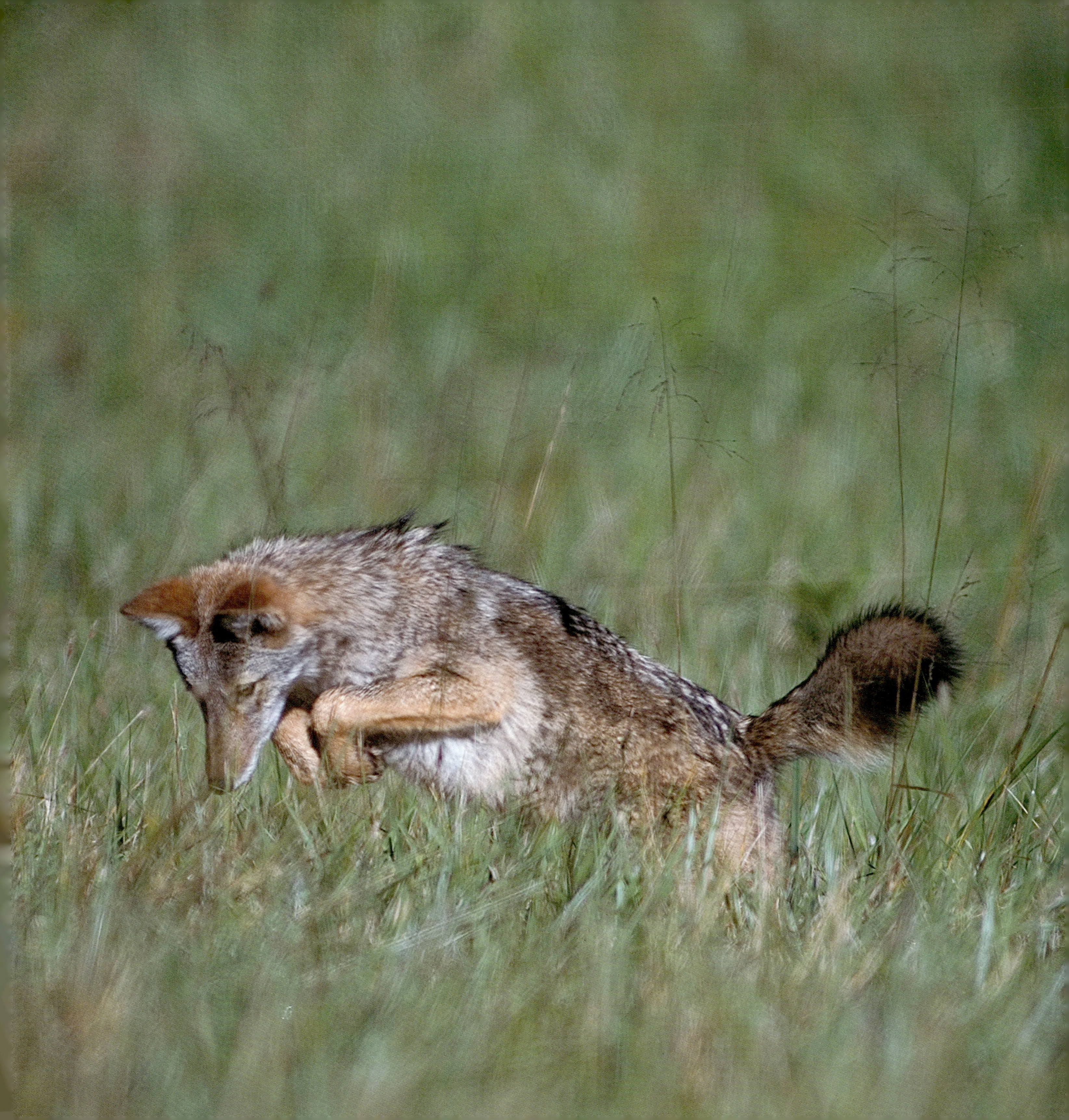

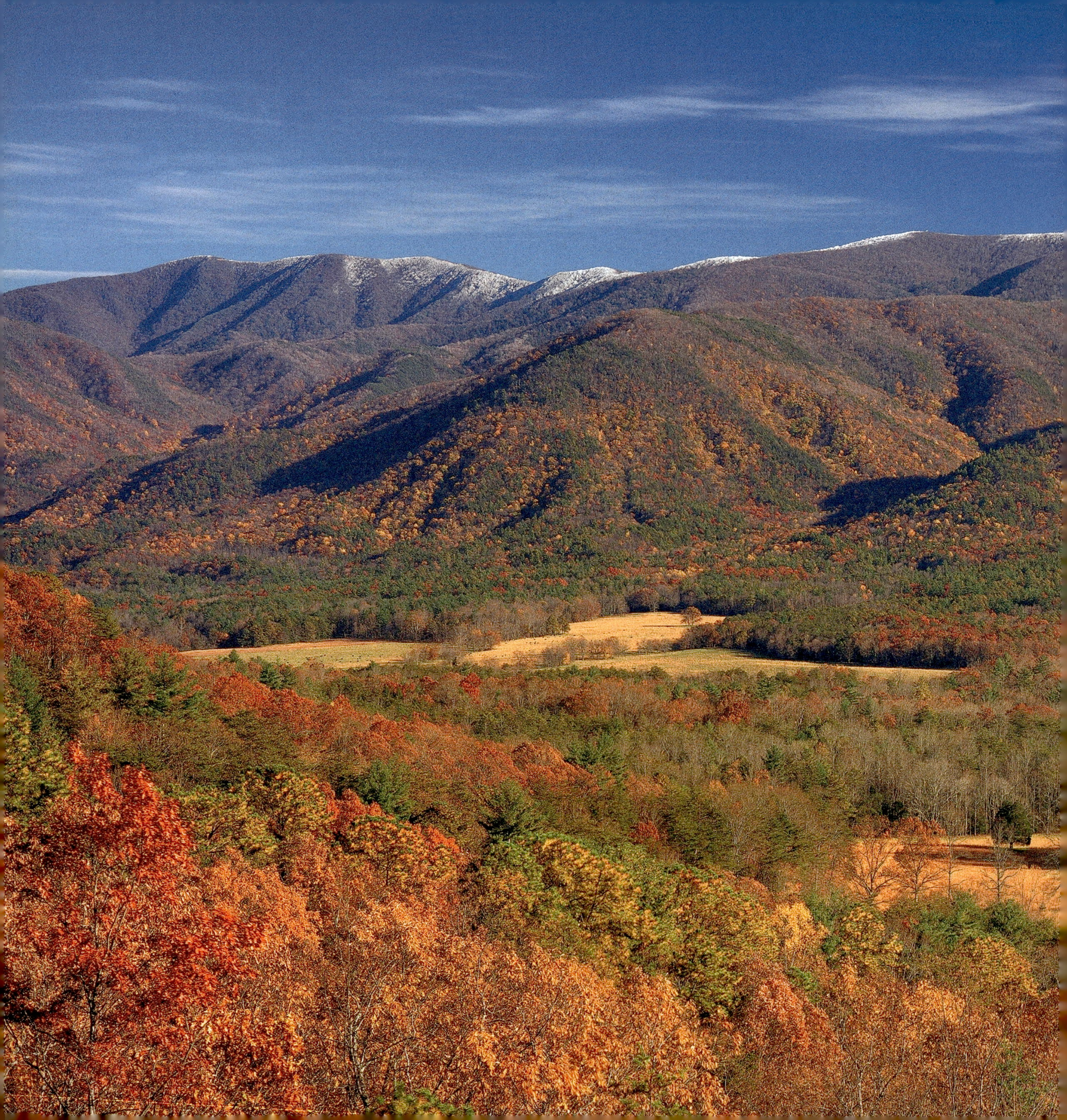

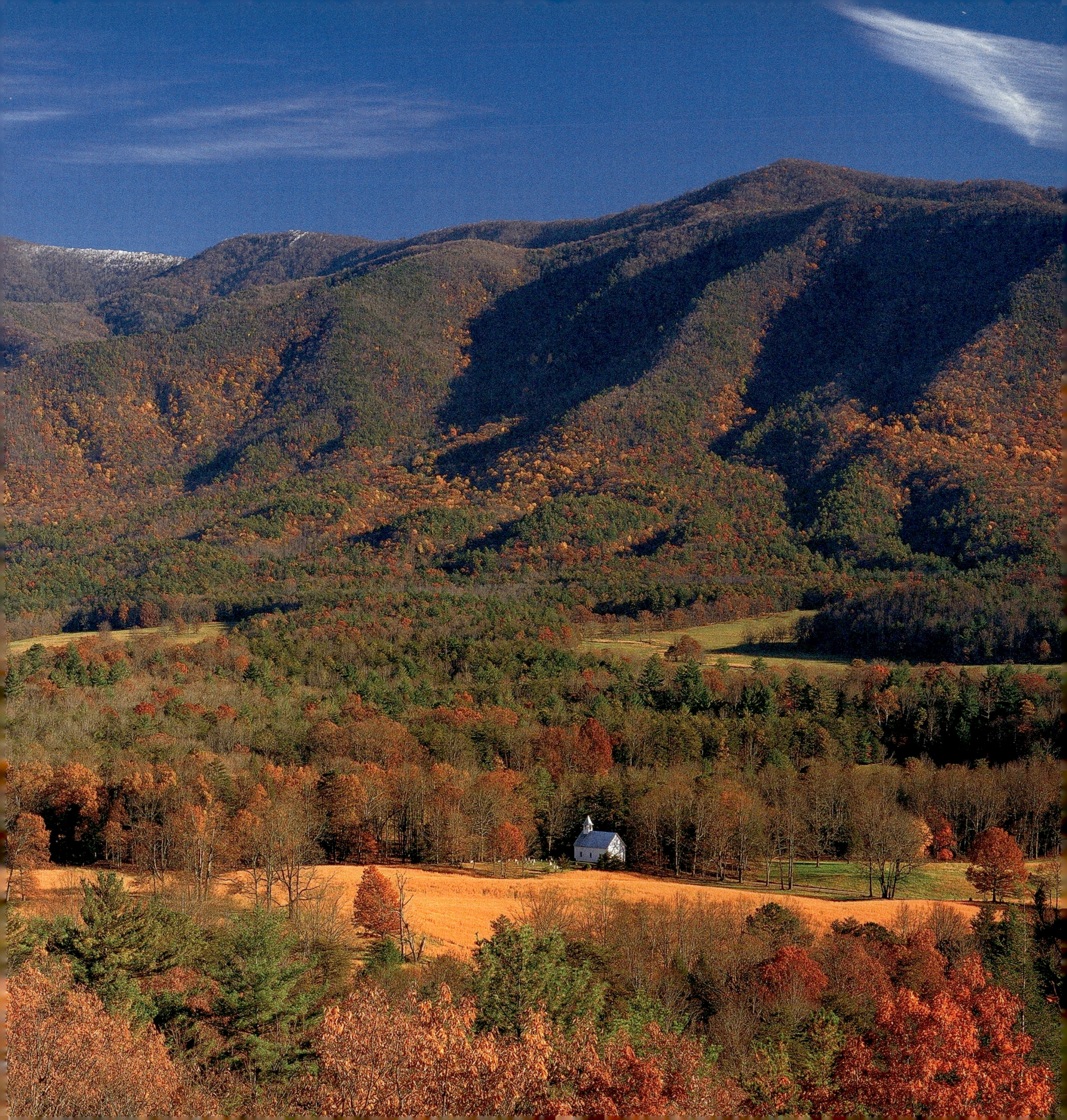

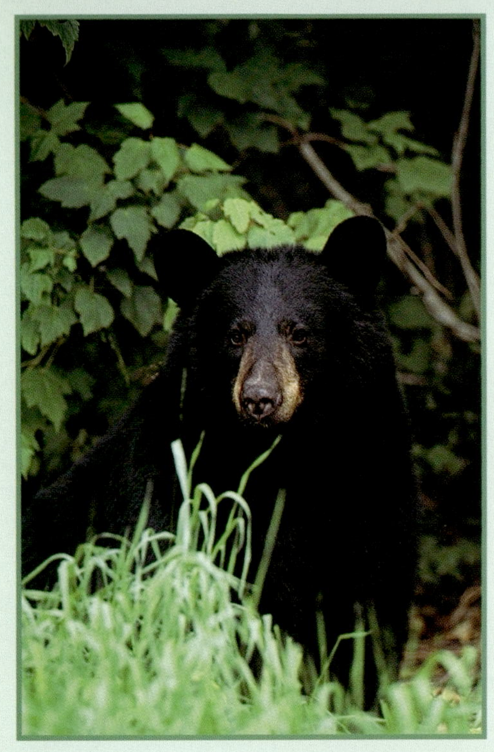
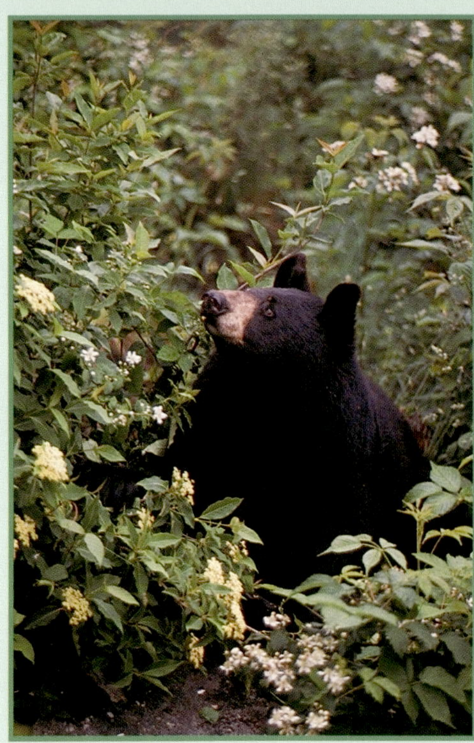
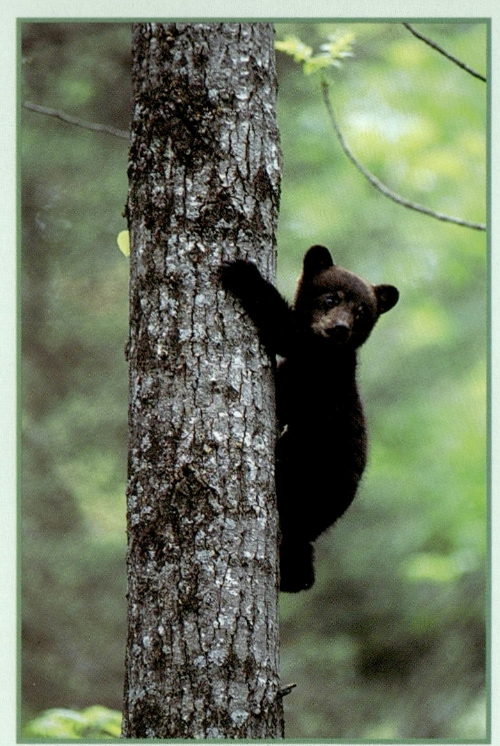

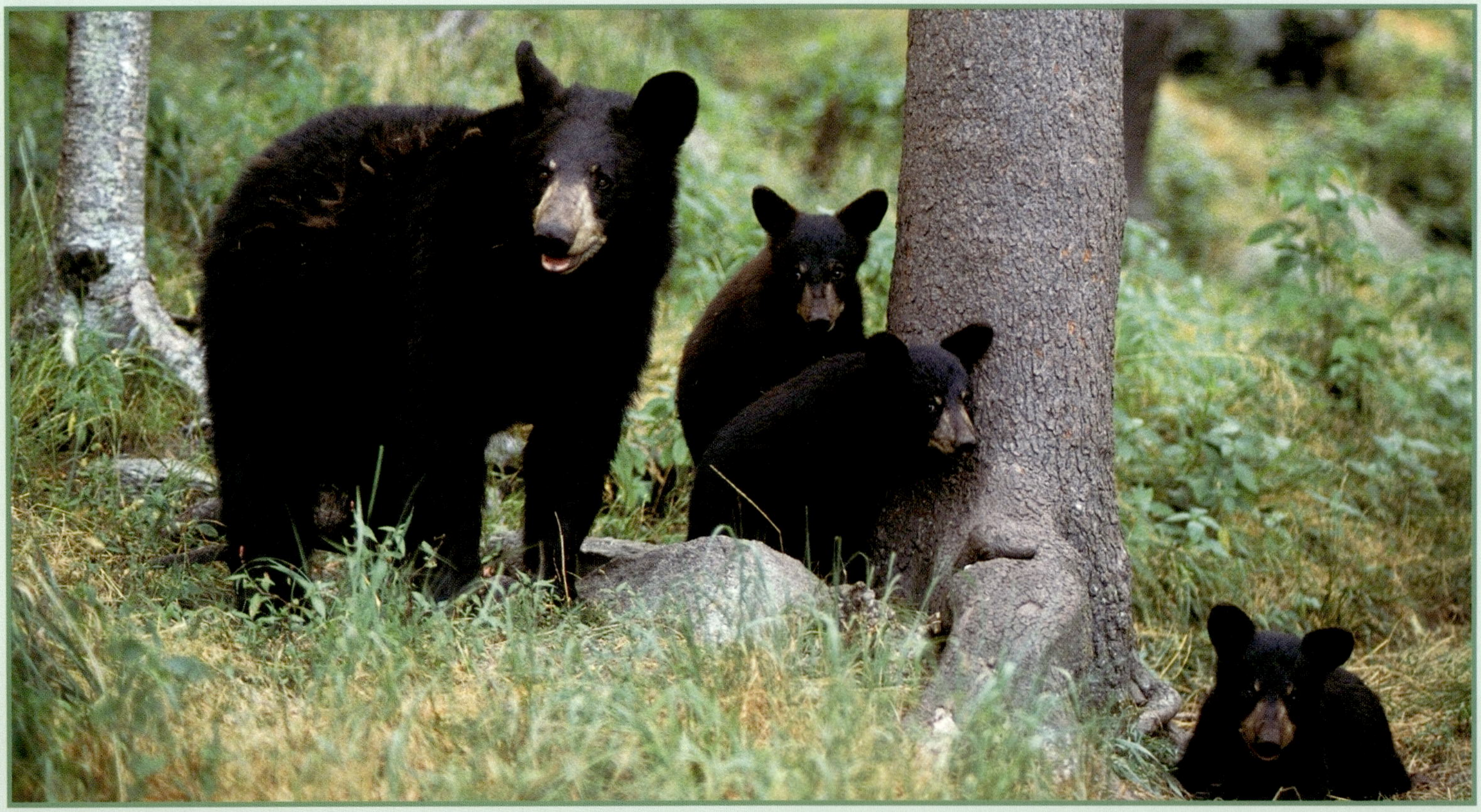

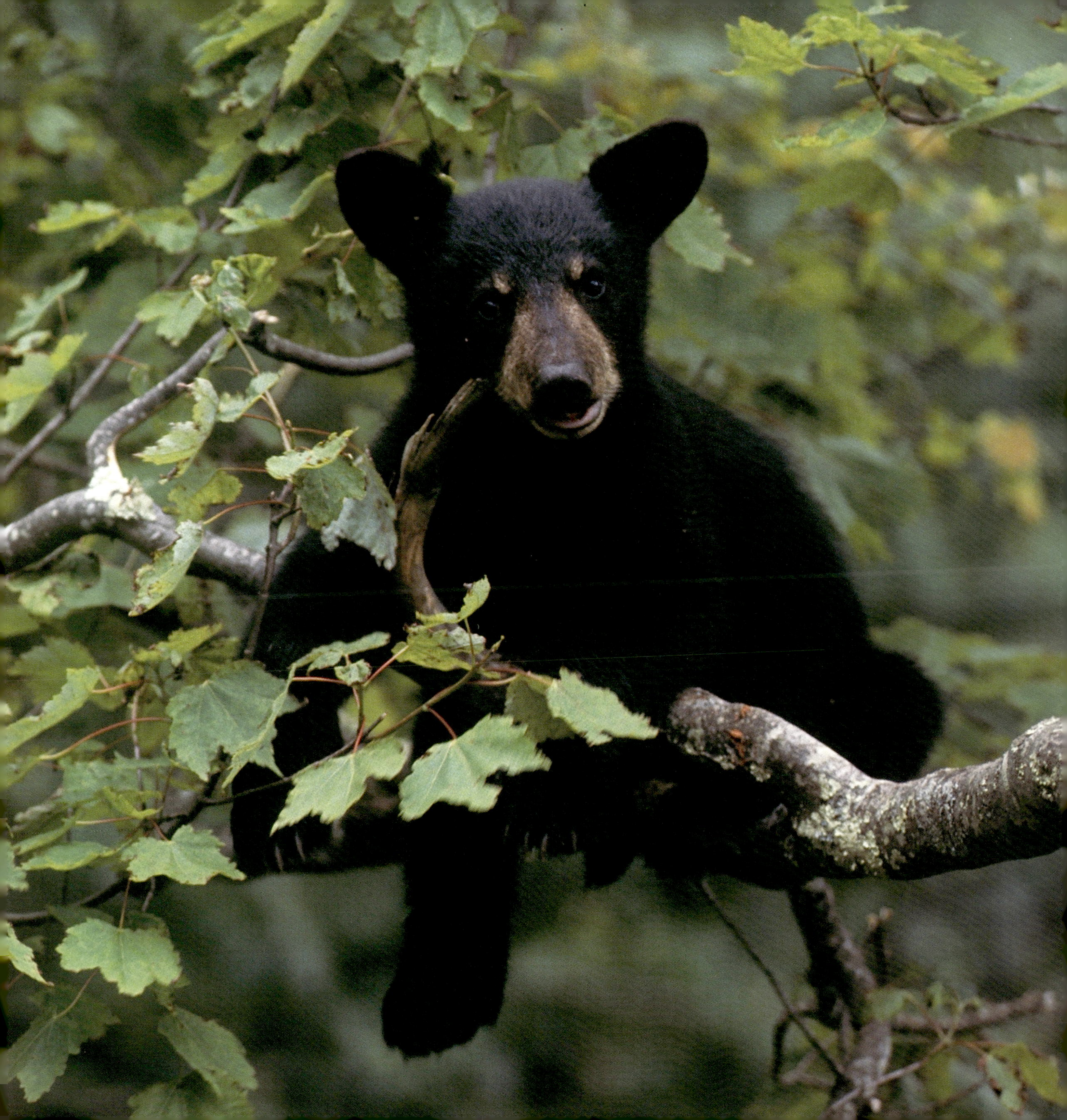

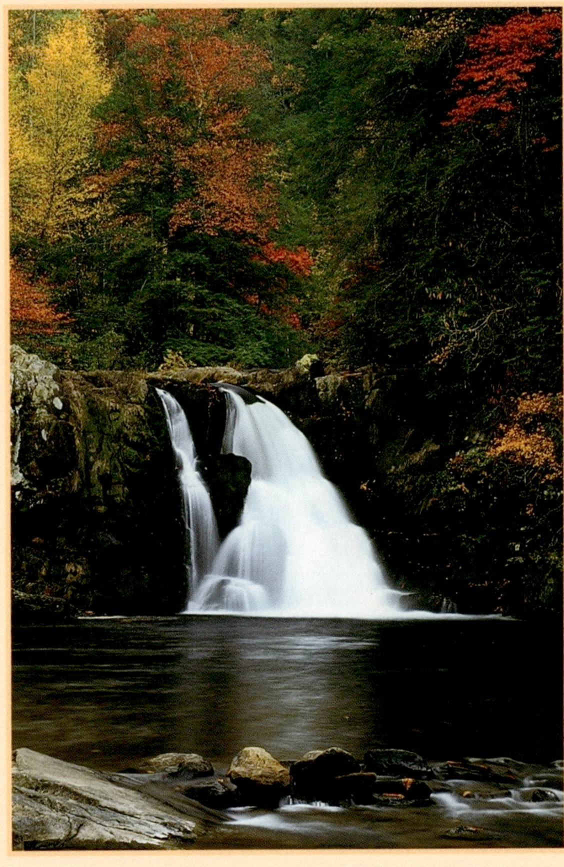

Above: Fall color above Abrams Falls, at the west end of Cades Cove (Bill Lea).

Right: Autumn comes to Middle Prong Little River, located in Tremont (Jerry Greer).

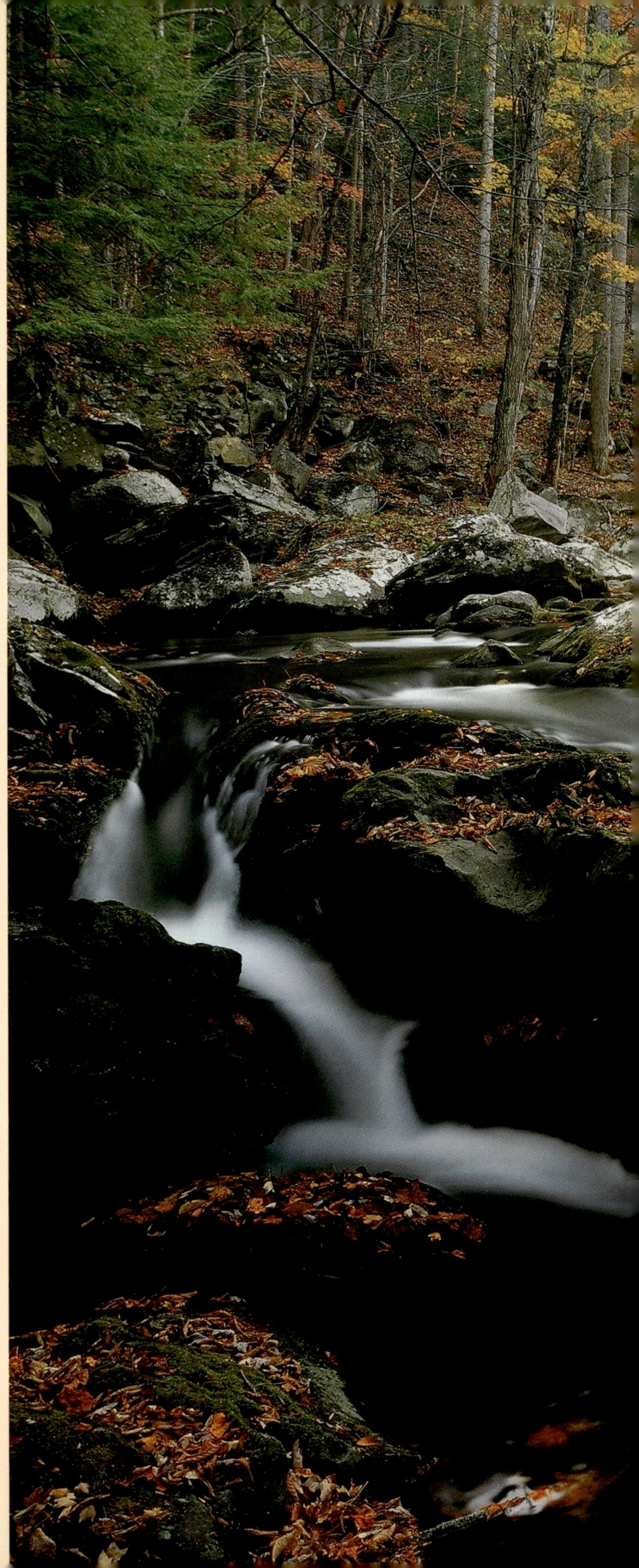

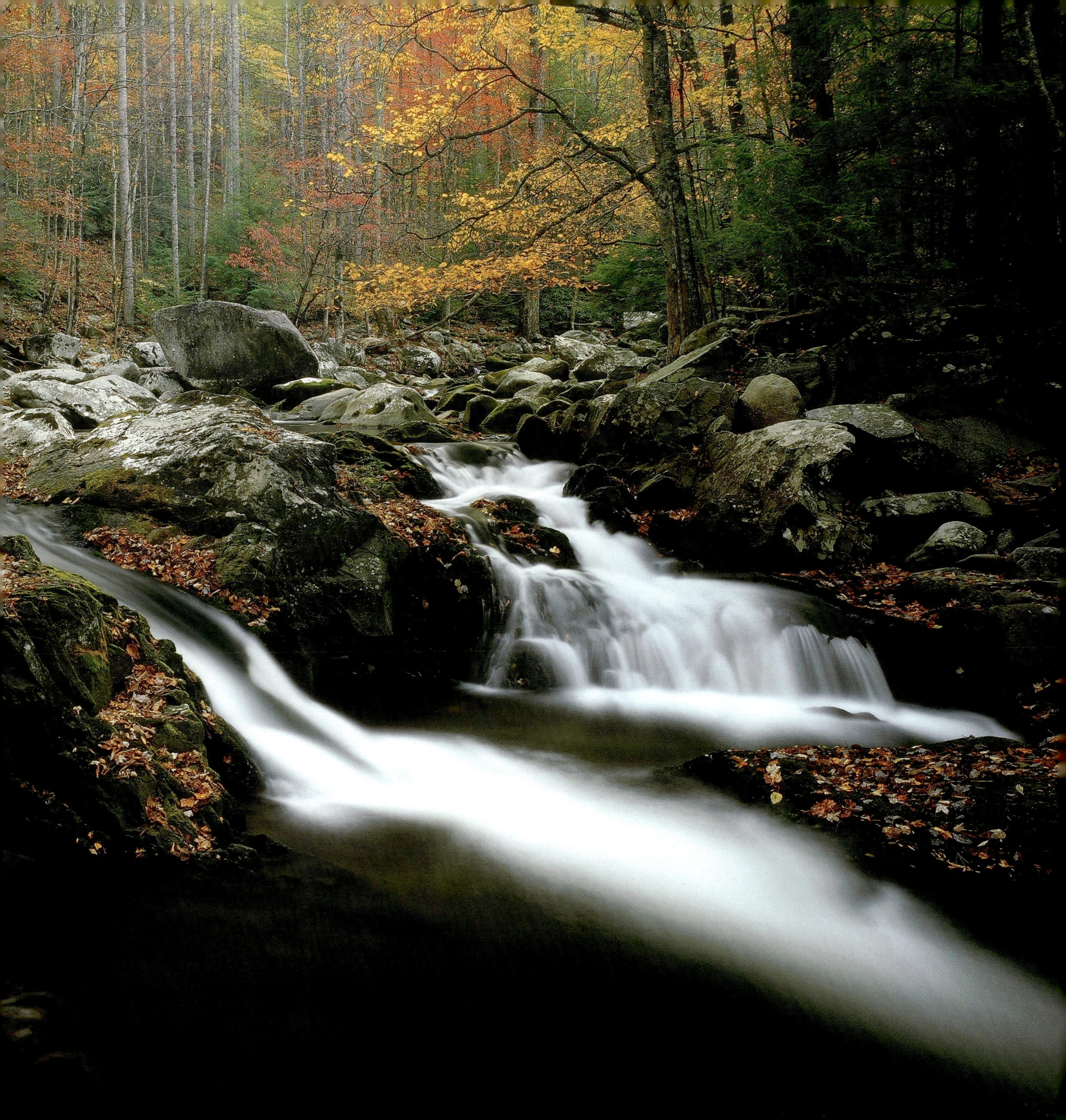

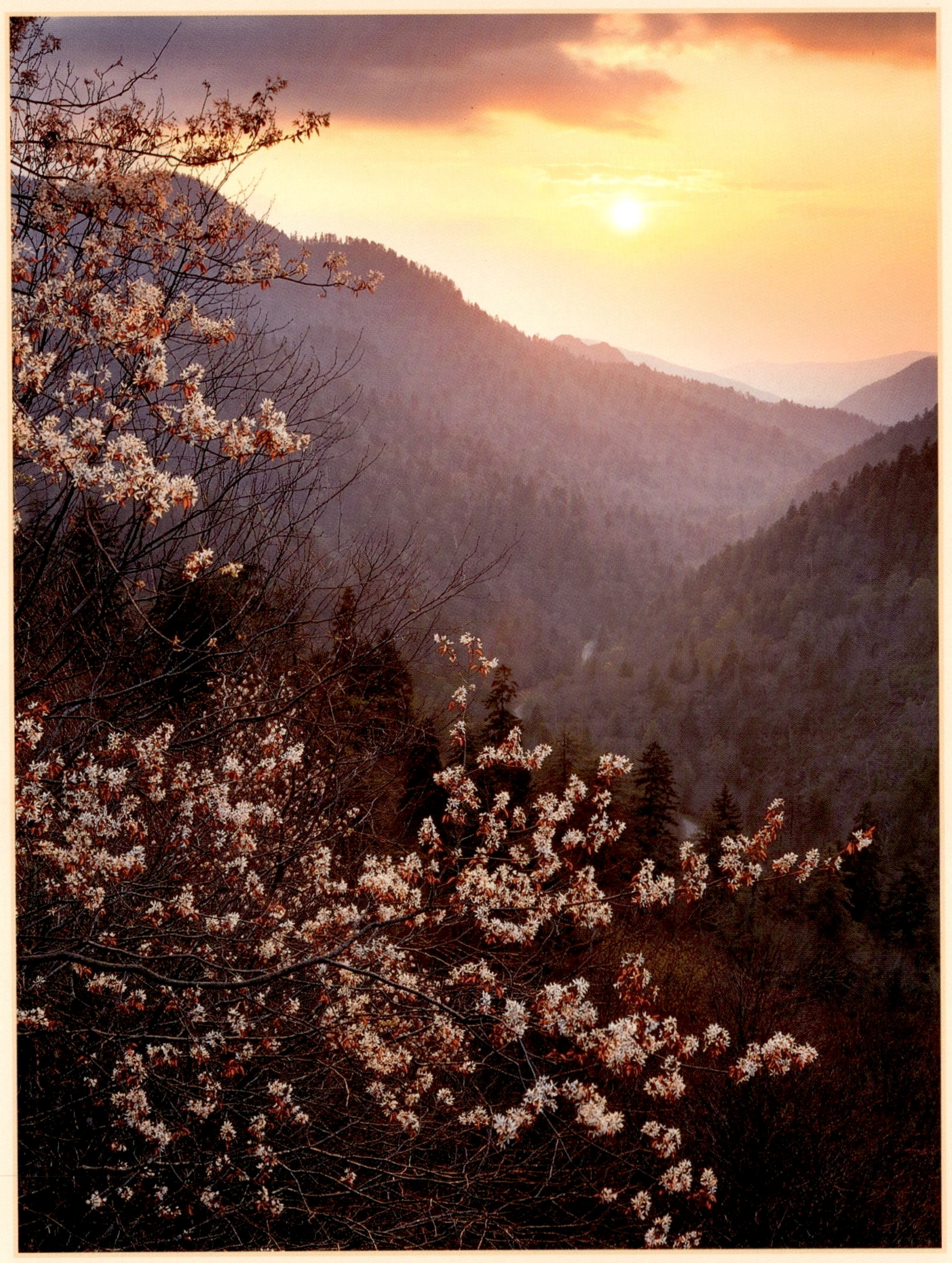

Sarvis tree blossoms frame the setting sun at Morton Overlook (Nye Simmons).

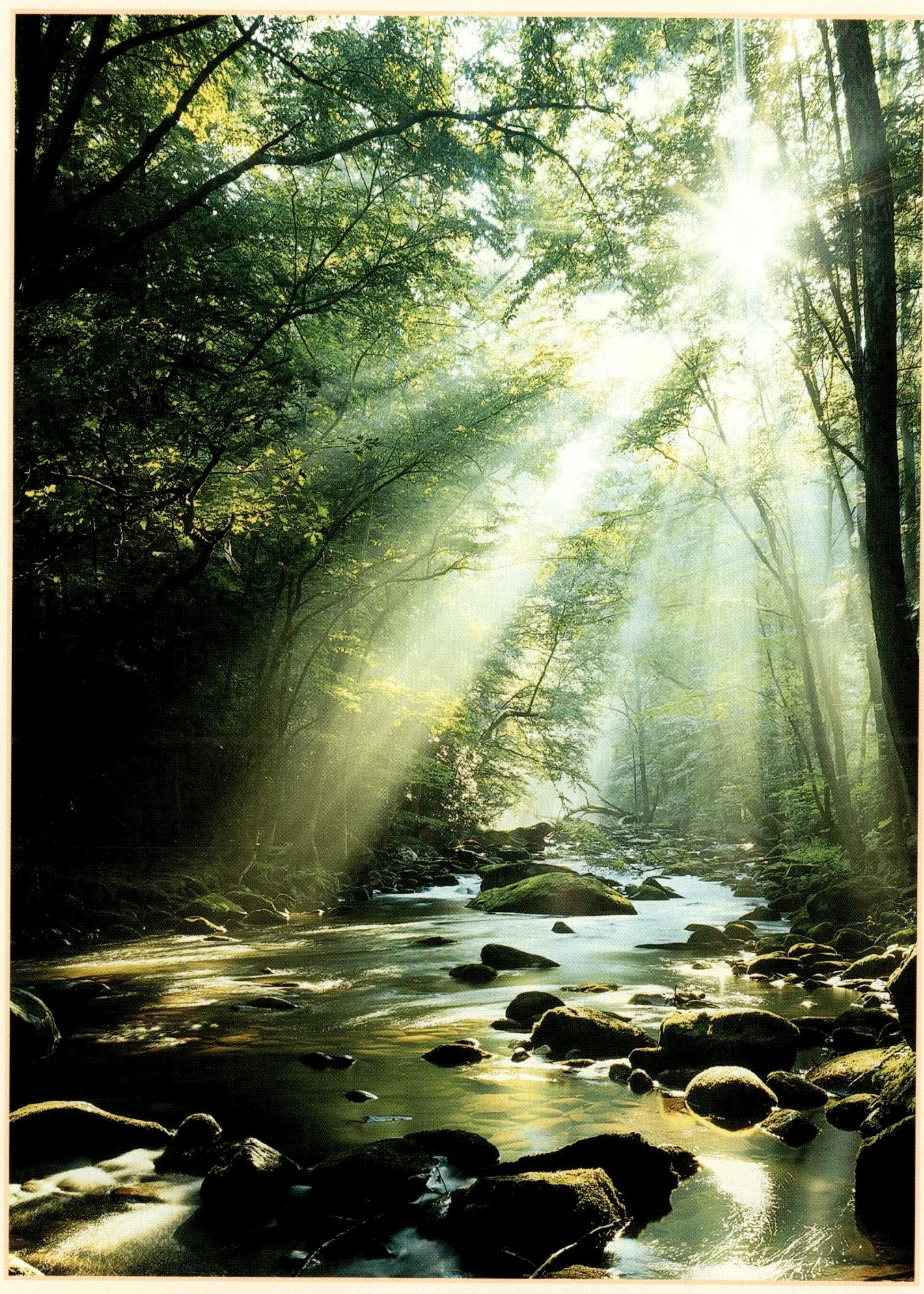

Sunbeams and morning light at Elkmont (Jerry Greer).

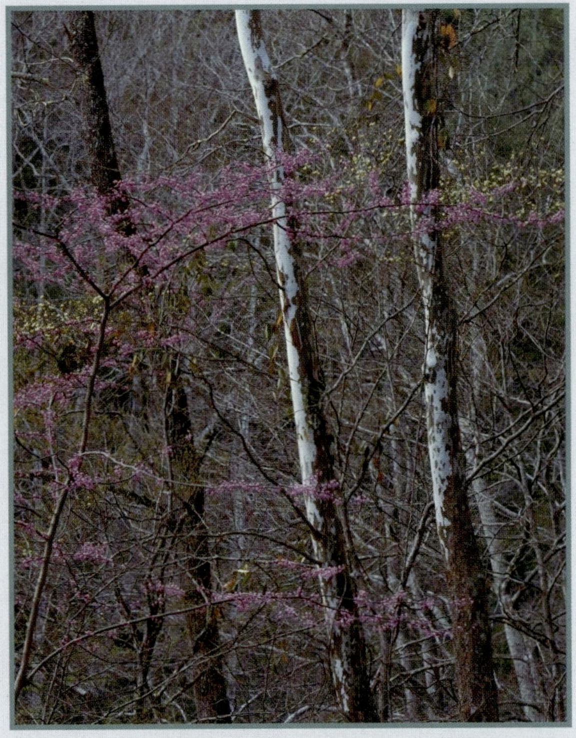

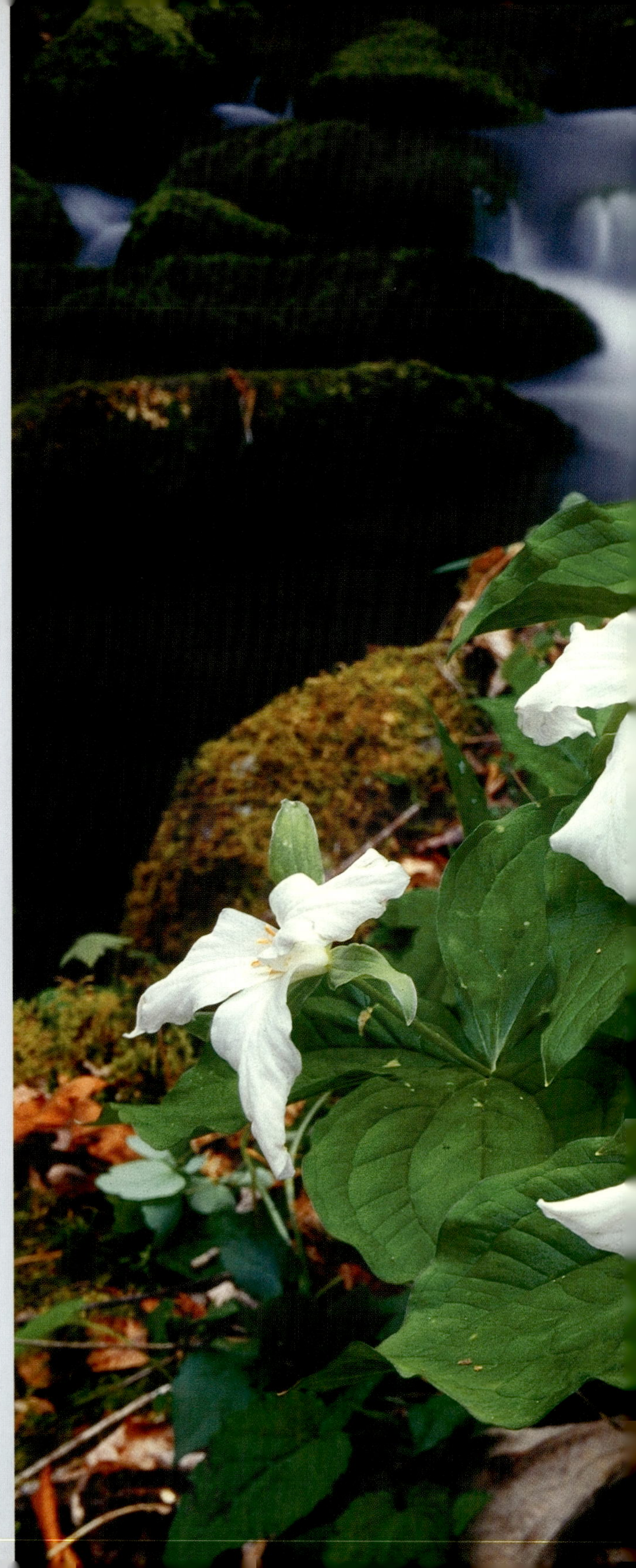

ONE OF THE SMOKIES' most beautiful floral displays occurs in spring when the trillium blooms. Found along many of the Park's streams and waterways, this delicate ephemeral lasts for only a short time (Jerry Greer).

Above: Redbud trees produce showy pink flowers in early spring (Nye Simmons).

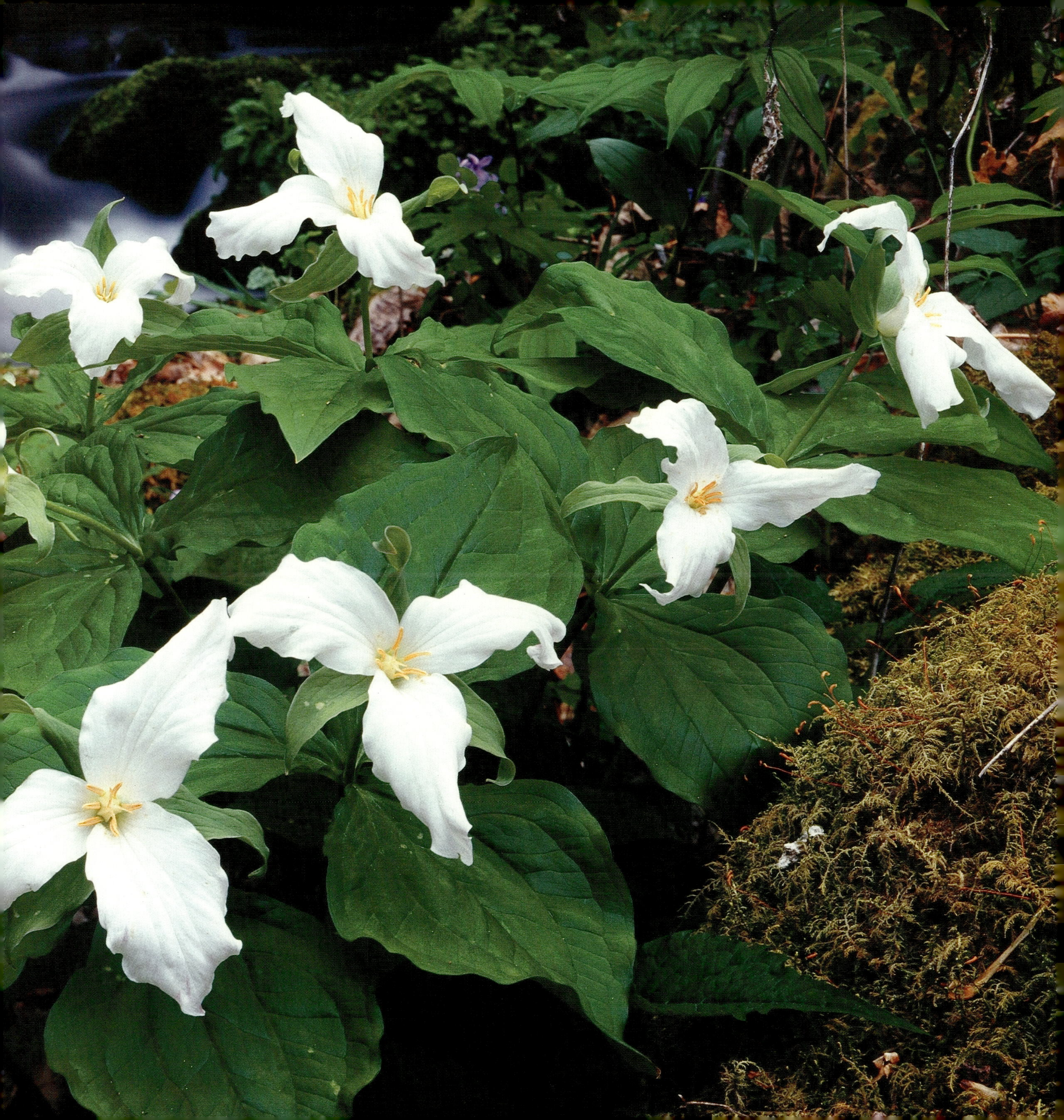

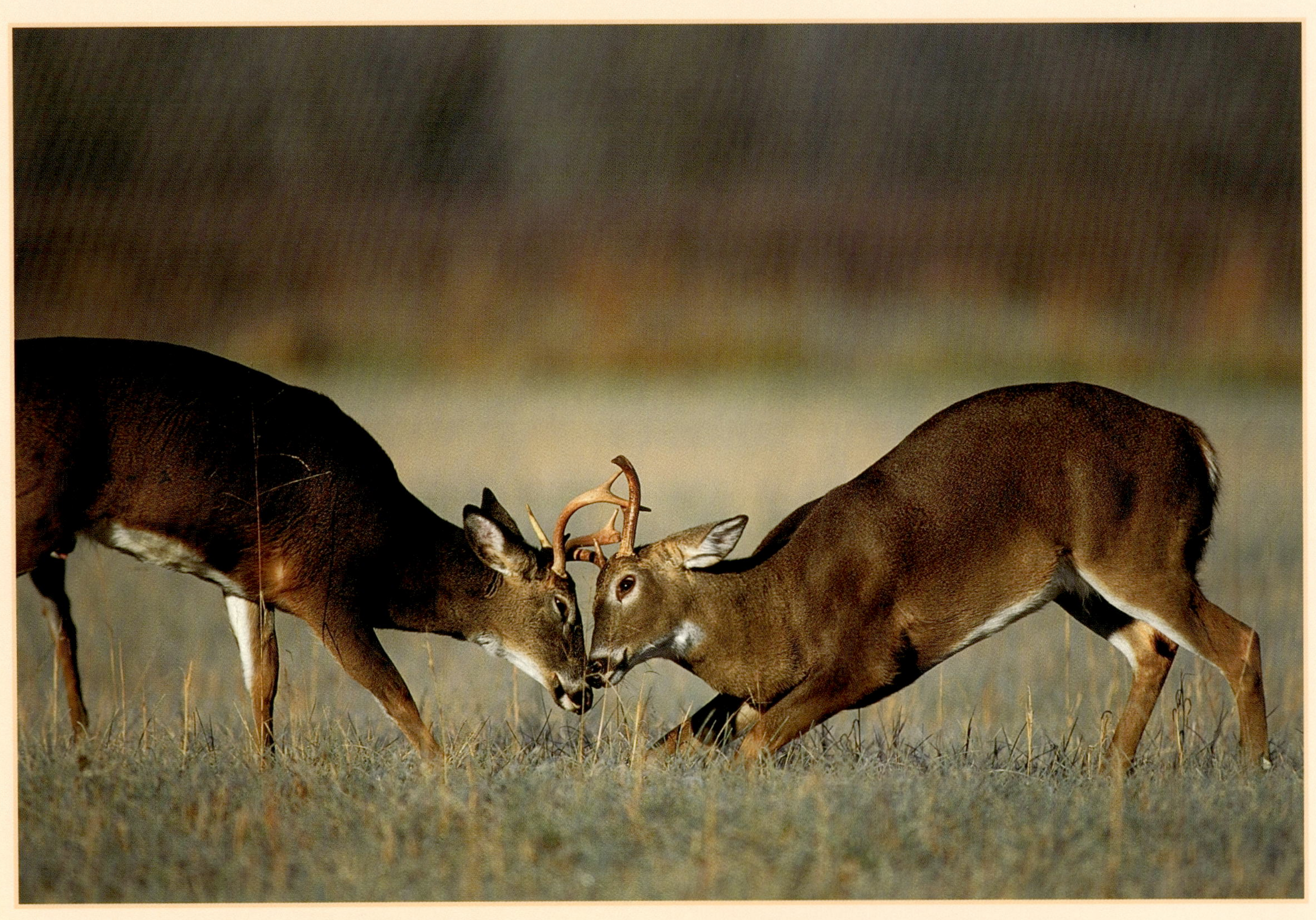

Two white-tailed deer bucks are locked in battle
during the fall rut (Bill Lea).

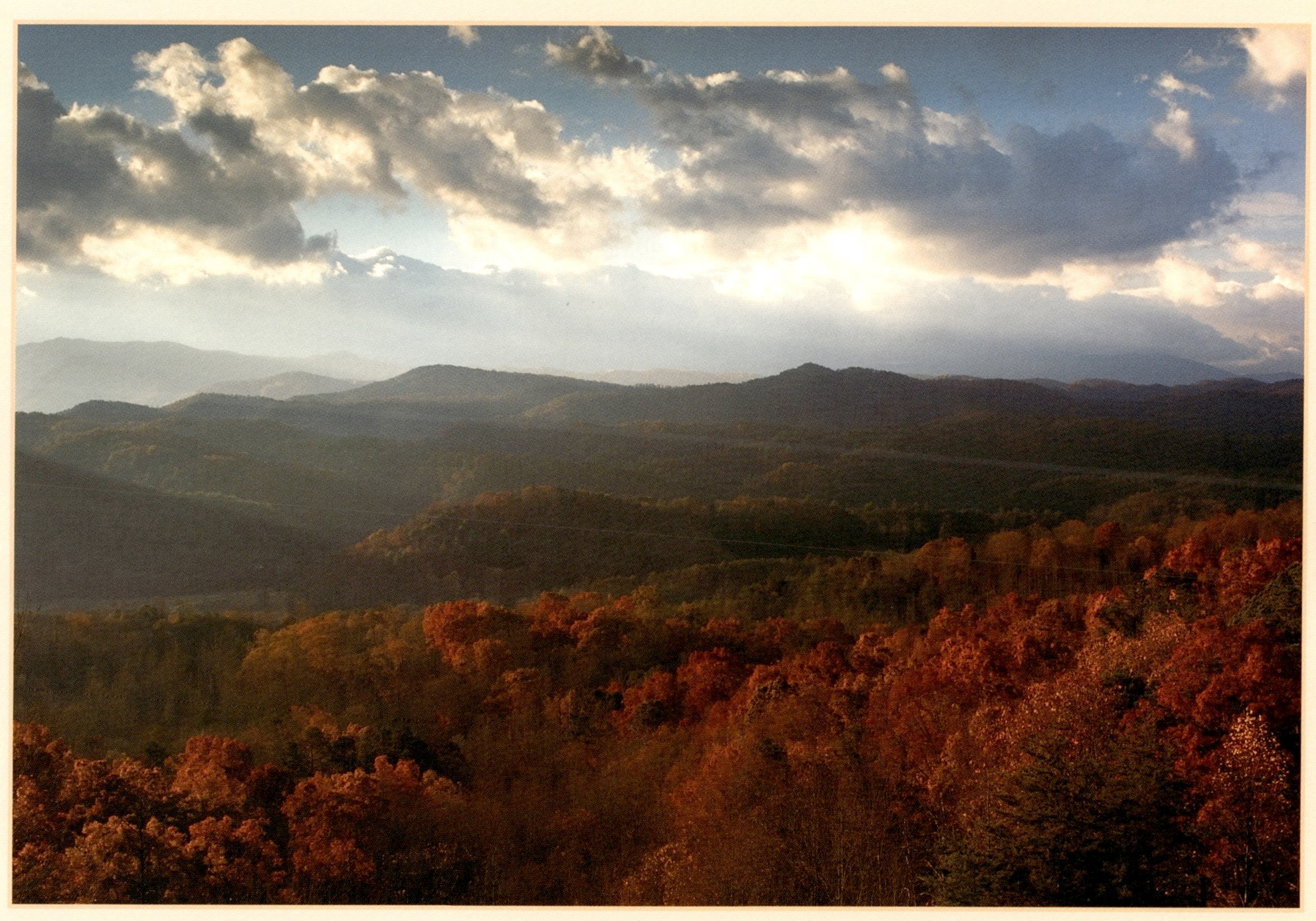

Dramatic clouds pass over autumn slopes (Bill Lea).

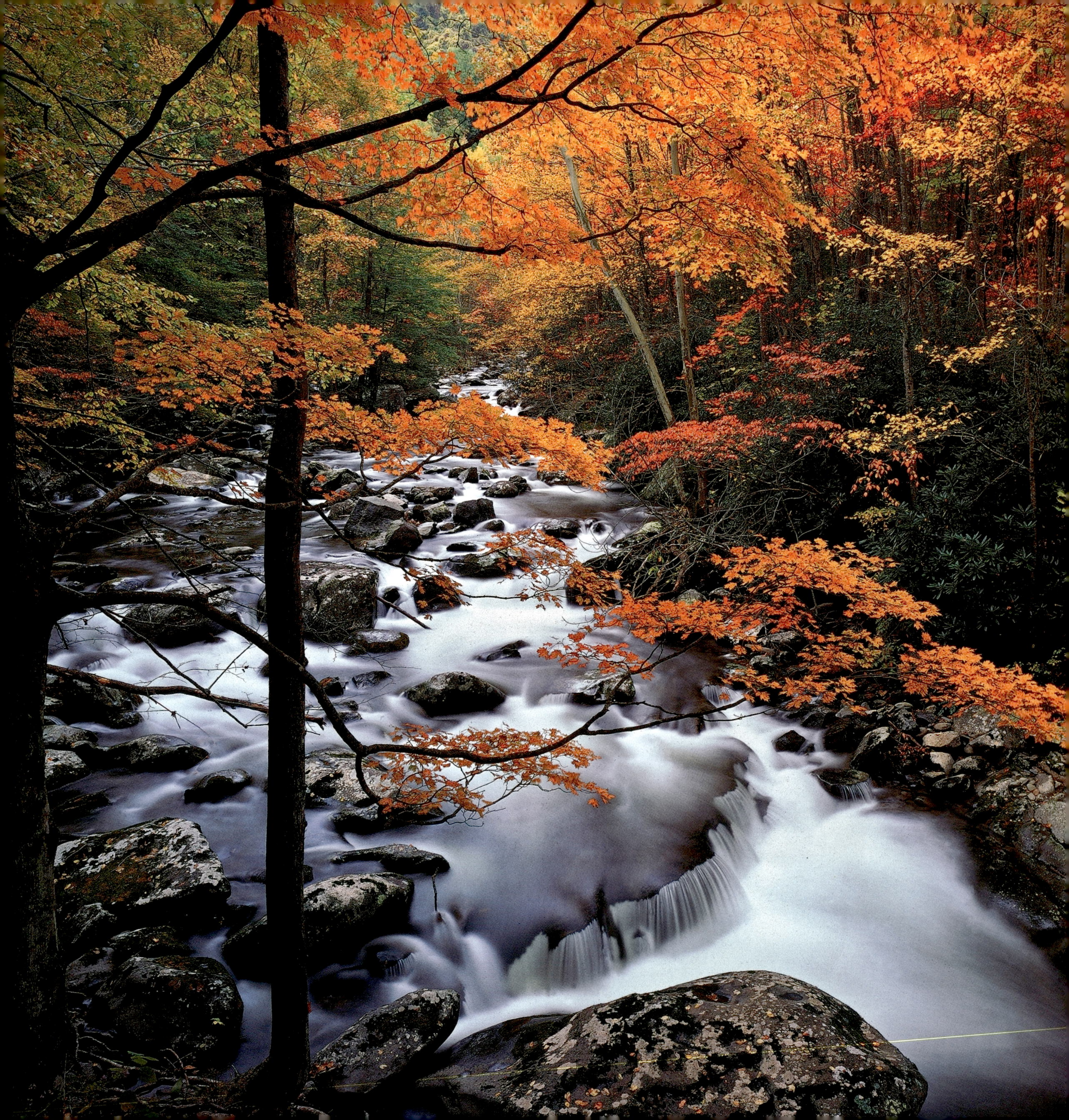

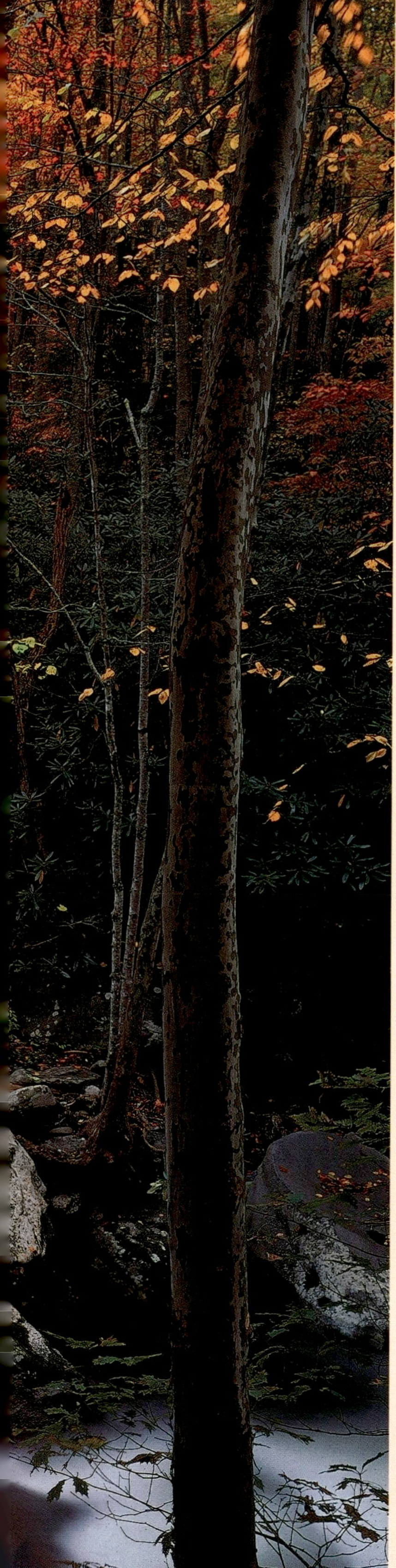

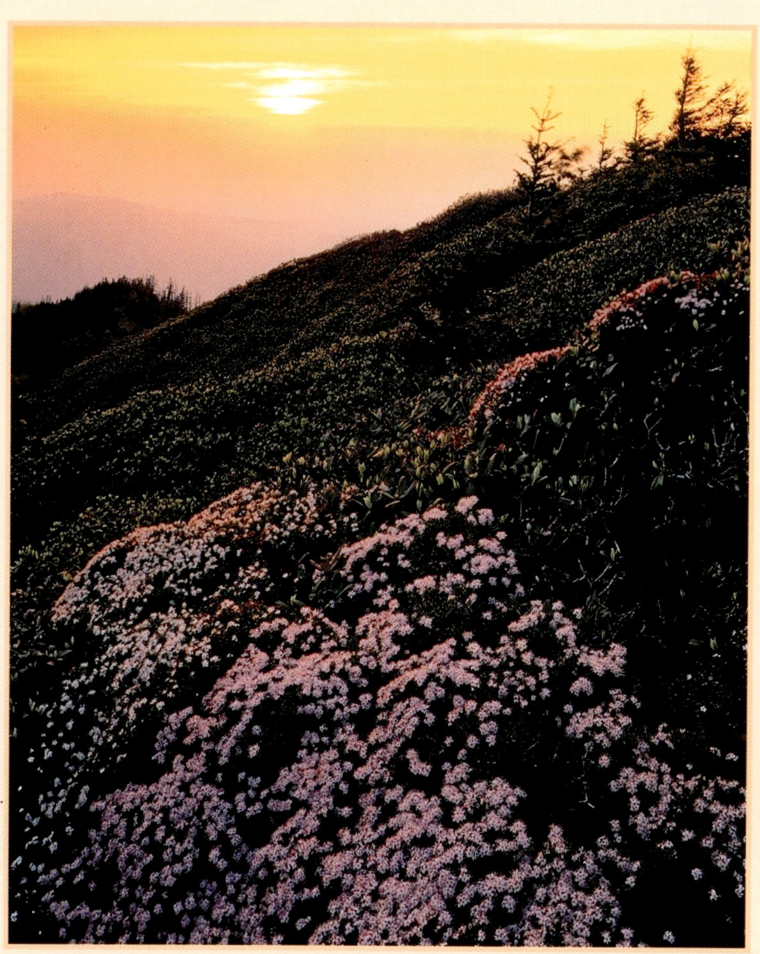

THE TREMONT AREA of the Smokies is a popular spot for viewing fall color. The Little River flows through this area, with tumbling cascades that mesmerize visitors – and photographers – alike (Nye Simmons).

Above: Myrtle blooms on the high altitude slopes of Mount Le Conte (Nye Simmons).

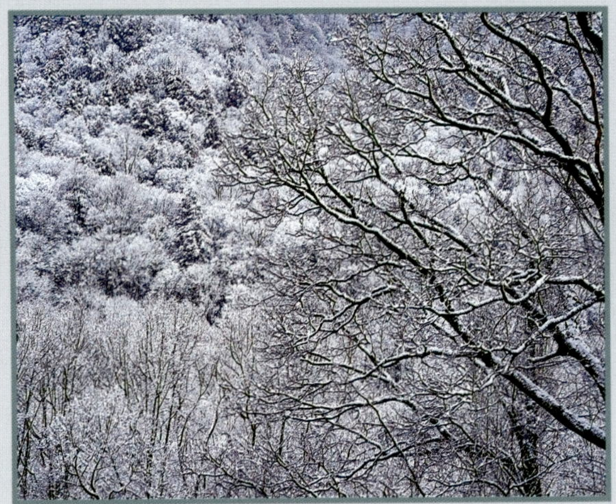

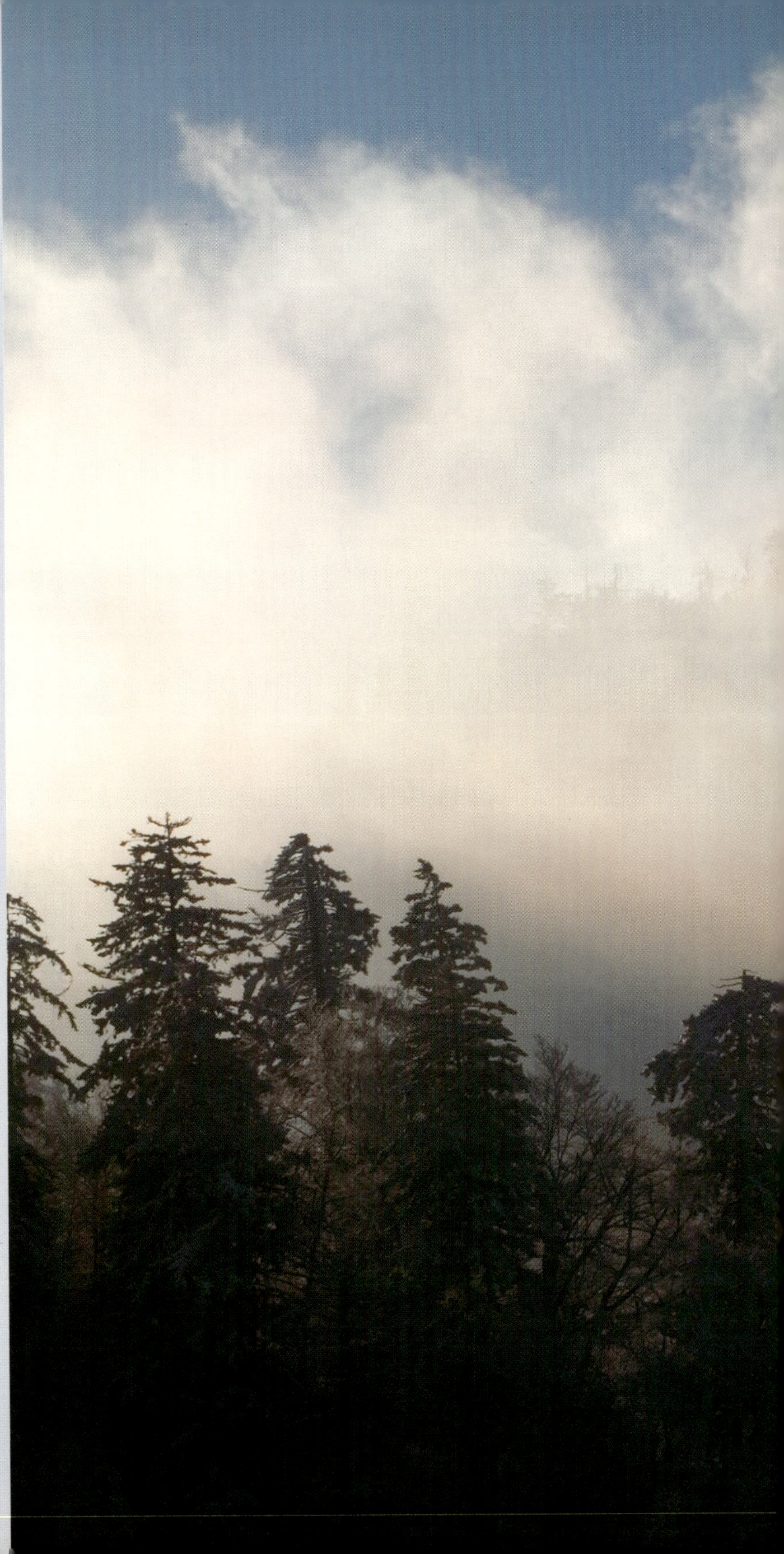

Above: Hoarfrost covers trees on the high slopes of the Smokies (Nye Simmons).

Right: After a winter storm, trees are covered in a sheath of icicles (Bill Lea).

Next page: Mountain laurel blooms along West Prong Little Pigeon River (Jerry Greer).

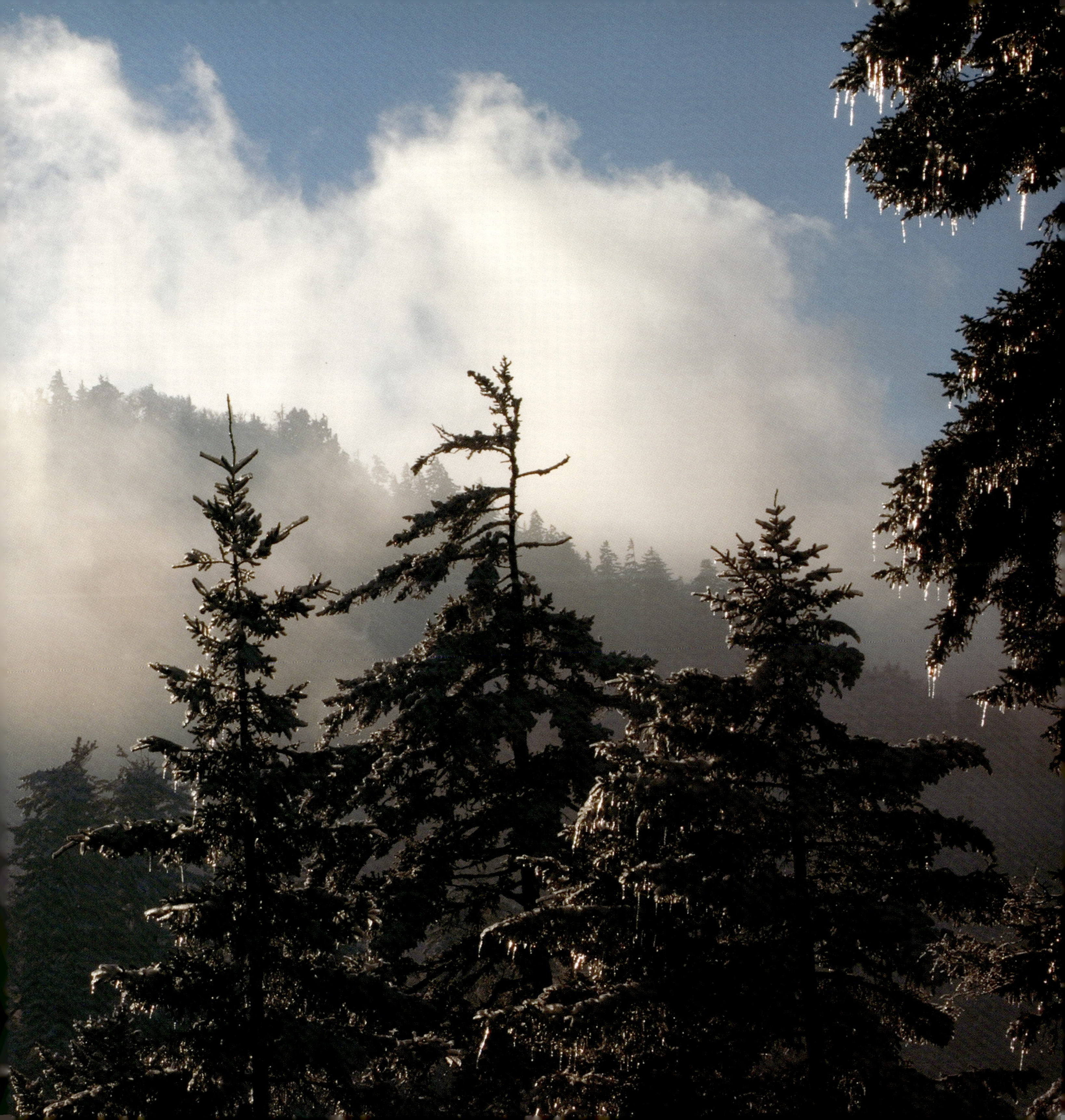

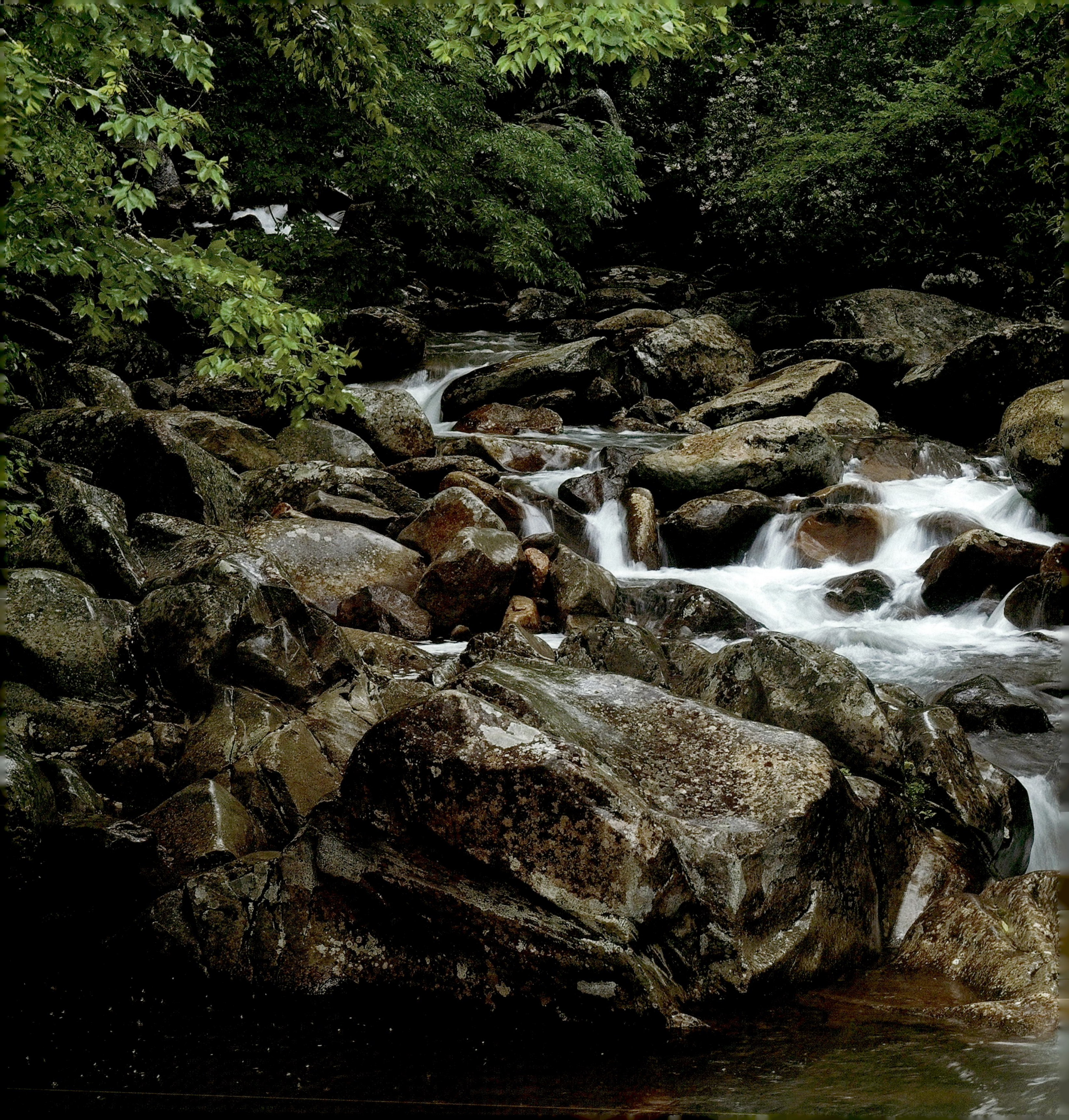

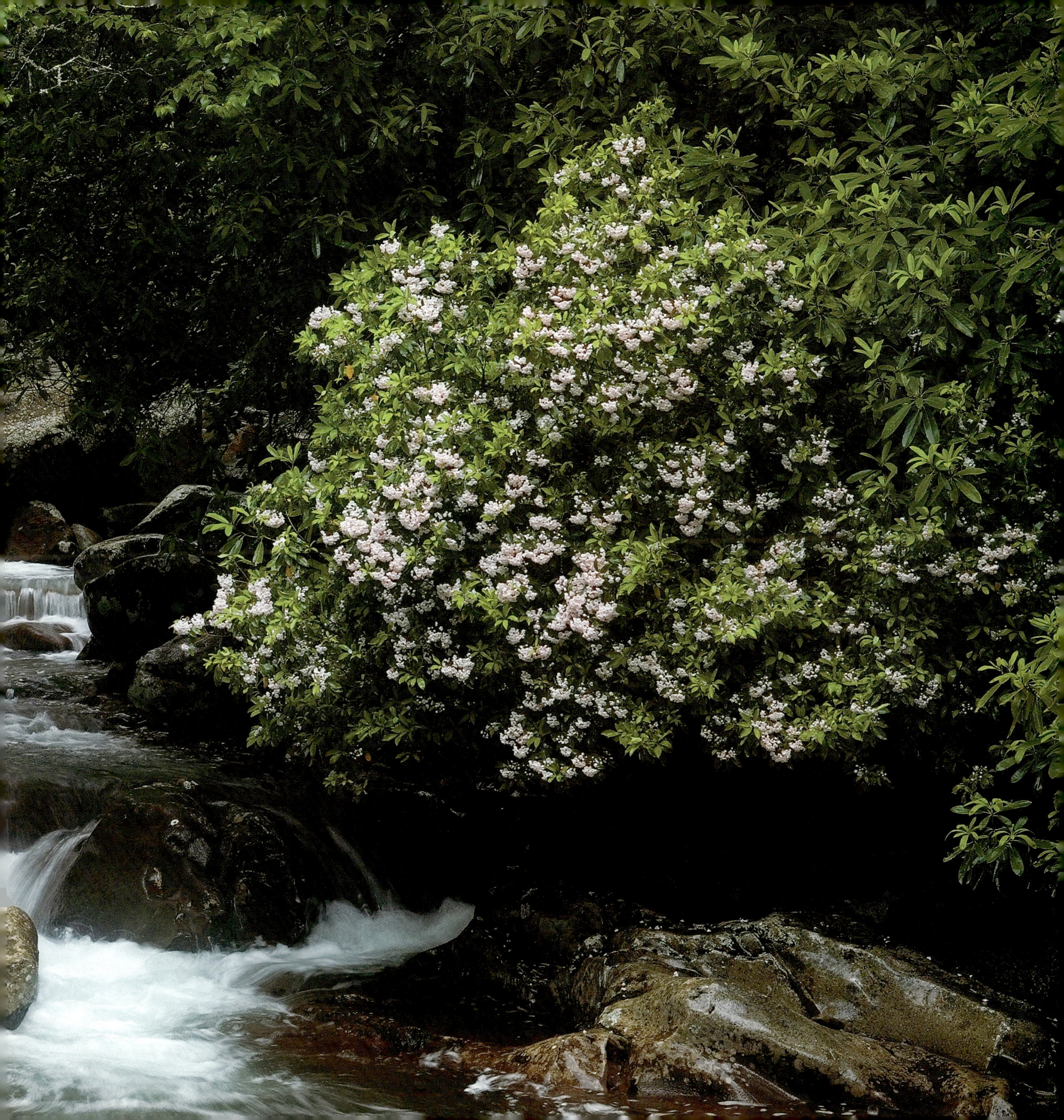

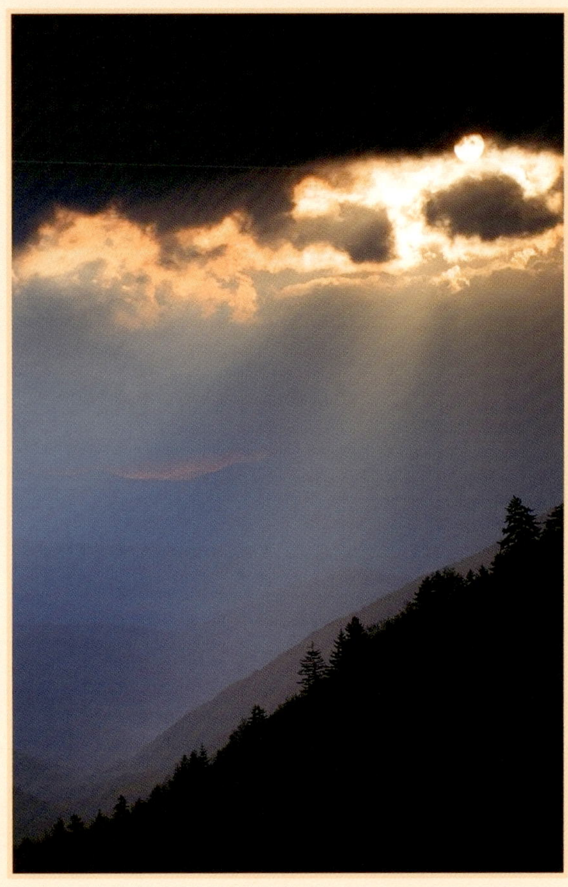

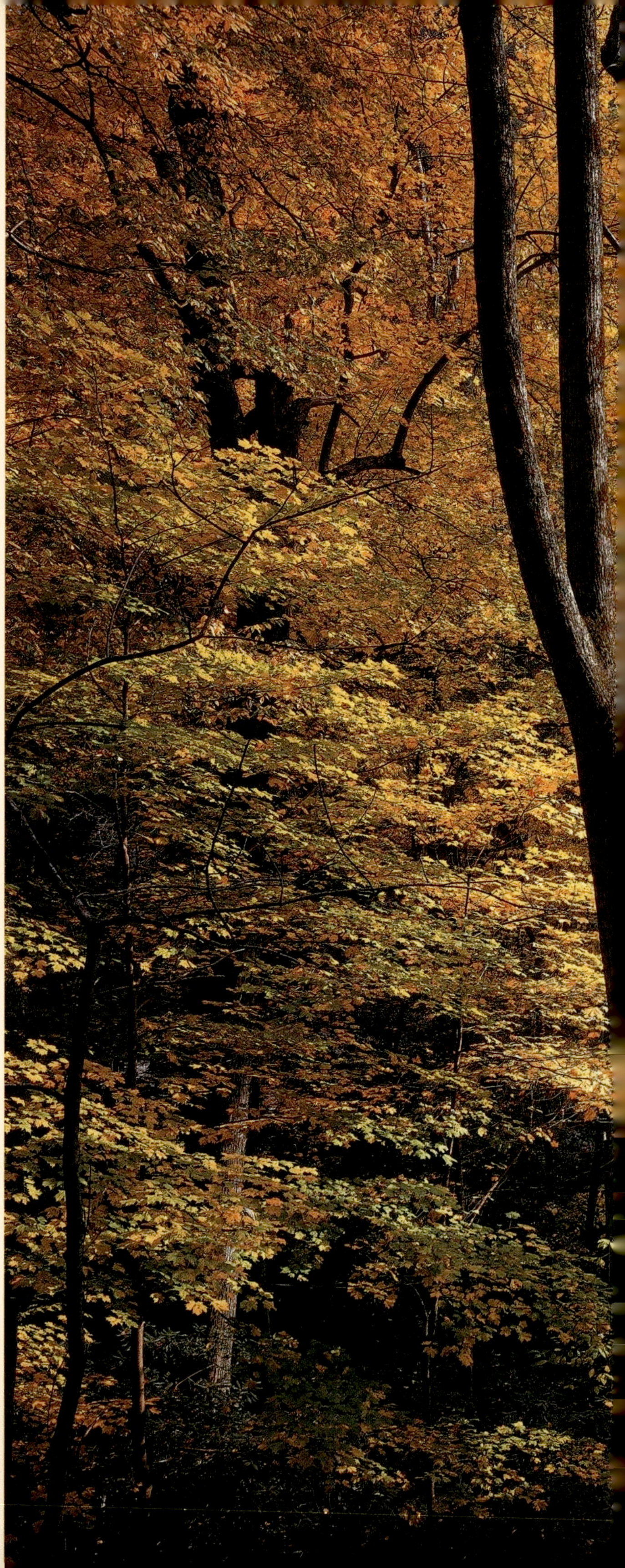

Above: A shaft of sunlight breaks through the clouds (Bill Lea).

Right: A symphony of color explodes in November in the lower elevations of the Smokies (Nye Simmons).

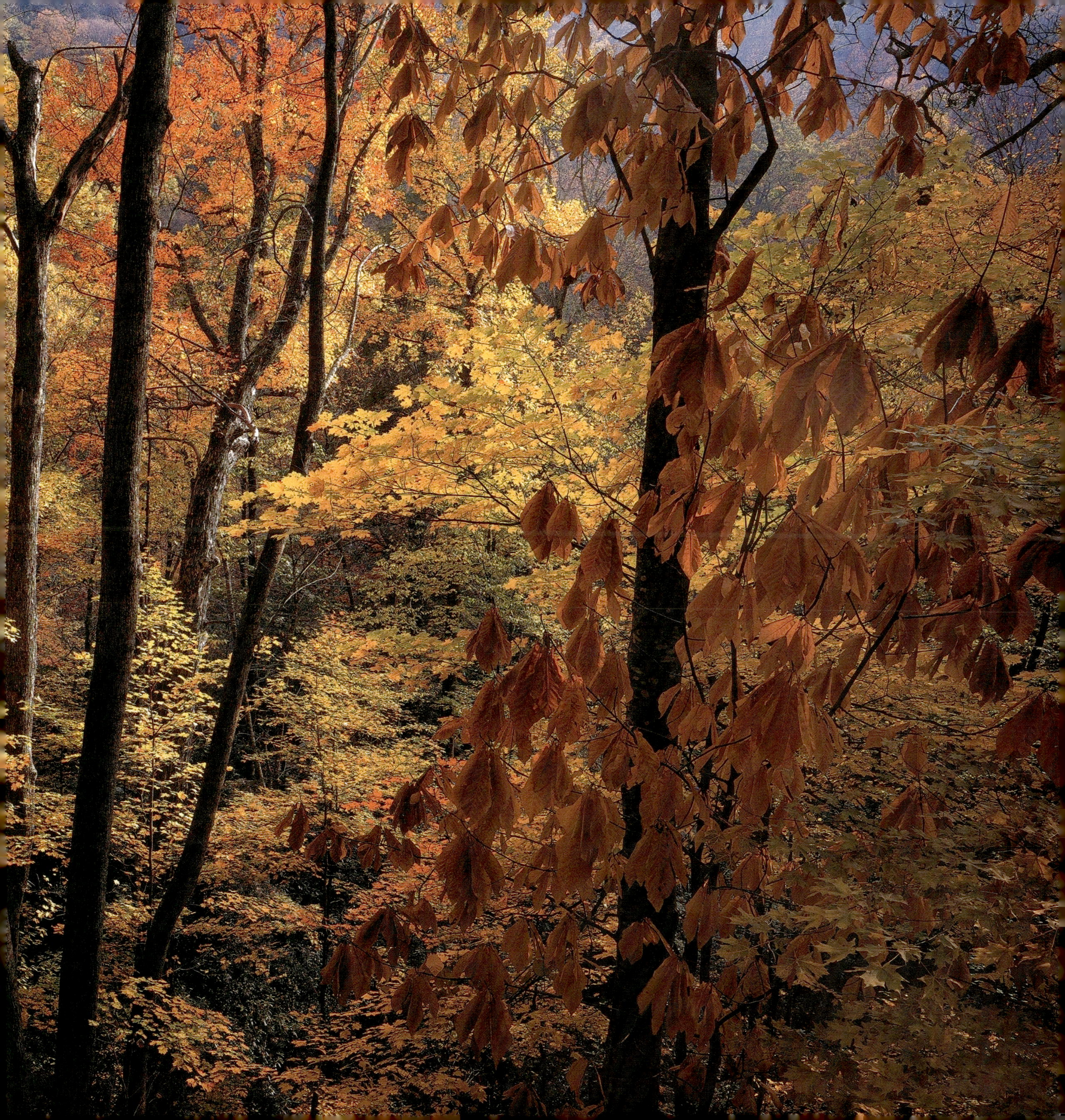

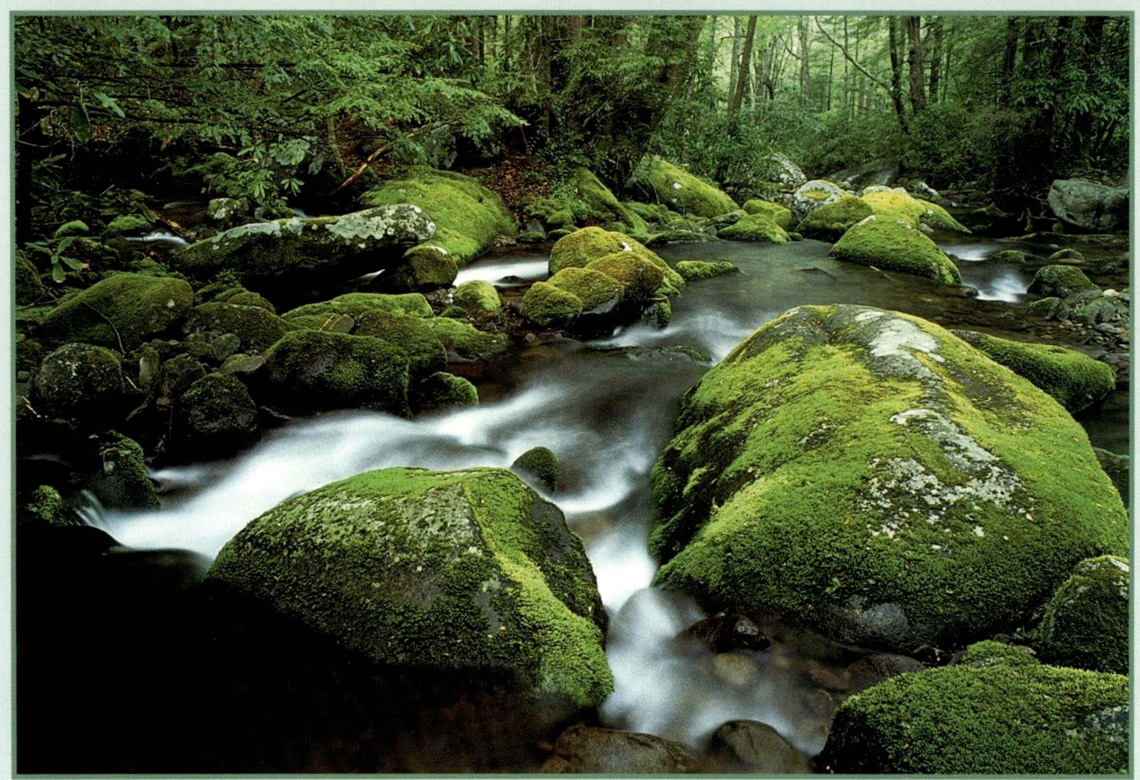

Above: Green moss covers boulders on the Roaring Fork (Bill Lea).

Back cover: A curious black bear cub sniffs the wind (Bill Lea).

About the Photographers:

Bill Lea has been photographing wildlife and nature since 1975. His work has appeared in a number of books and publications. He has lived with his wife Klari in the Smoky Mountain region since 1983. His images can be viewed on his website **www.billlea.com**.

Jerry D. Greer has been photographing our scenic and natural places for over fifteen years. His work has appeared in a number of books and publications, including seven other books by Mountain Trail Press. He lives in Johnson City, Tennessee with his wife Angela. His images can be viewed on his website **www.jerrygreerphotography.com**.

Nye Simmons has been capturing special natural moments on film since the 1980s. His work has appeared in a number of books and publications, including one other book by Mountain Trail Press. He lives in Knoxville, Tennessee with his wife Deborah. His images can be viewed on his website at **www.simmonphotoarts.com**.

Other Books by Mountain Trail Press in the *Wonder and Light* series:

Shenandoah Wonder and Light
Virginia Wonder and Light
West Virginia Wonder and Light
Blue Ridge Parkway Wonder and Light
Washington, D.C. Wonder and Light
North Carolina Wonder and Light
Tennessee Wonder and Light
South Carolina Wonder and Light
Maryland Wonder and Light